MW00962960

Learning Nessus for Penetration Testing

Master how to perform IT infrastructure security vulnerability assessments using Nessus with tips and insights from real-world challenges faced during vulnerability assessment

Himanshu Kumar

BIRMINGHAM - MUMBAI

Learning Nessus for Penetration Testing

Copyright © 2014 Packt Publishing

All rights reserved. No part of this book may be reproduced, stored in a retrieval system, or transmitted in any form or by any means, without the prior written permission of the publisher, except in the case of brief quotations embedded in critical articles or reviews.

Every effort has been made in the preparation of this book to ensure the accuracy of the information presented. However, the information contained in this book is sold without warranty, either express or implied. Neither the author, nor Packt Publishing, and its dealers and distributors will be held liable for any damages caused or alleged to be caused directly or indirectly by this book.

Packt Publishing has endeavored to provide trademark information about all of the companies and products mentioned in this book by the appropriate use of capitals. However, Packt Publishing cannot guarantee the accuracy of this information.

First published: January 2014

Production Reference: 1170114

Published by Packt Publishing Ltd.
Livery Place
35 Livery Street
Birmingham B3 2PB, UK.

ISBN 978-1-78355-099-9

www.packtpub.com

Cover Image by Paul Steven (mediakitchenuk@gmail.com)

Credits

Author
Himanshu Kumar

Reviewers
Veerendra GG
Martin MacLorrain Jr.

Acquisition Editors
Kevin Colaco
Andrew Duckworth

Commissioning Editor
Deepika Singh

Technical Editors
Novina Kewalramani
Amit Ramadas
Amit Shetty

Copy Editors
Alisha Aranha
Brandt D'Mello
Tanvi Gaitonde
Shambhavi Pai
Laxmi Subramanian

Project Coordinator
Sageer Parkar

Proofreader
Paul Hindle

Indexer
Hemangini Bari

Graphics
Yuvraj Mannari

Production Coordinator
Nilesh Bambardekar

Cover Work
Nilesh Bambardekar

About the Author

Himanshu Kumar is a very passionate security specialist with multiple years of experience as a security researcher. He has hands-on experience in almost all domains of Information Security specializing in Vulnerability Assessment and Penetration Testing. He enjoys writing scripts to exploit vulnerabilities. He is active on different security forums, such as webappsec and securityfocus where he loves responding to different security problems.

Every book goes in many hands before it is published. The real credit goes to their work which makes publishing a book possible. Without the efforts being put in by the Packt editing team, the Packt publishing team, technical editors, and reviewers, this would have not been possible. I would like to extend my sincere gratitude to the Packt team Yogesh Dalvi, Sageer Parkar, Deepika Singh, Kevin Colaco, Novina Kewalramani, Sumeet Sawant, and the reviewers Martin MacLorrain Jr. and Veerendra GG.

I would also like to thank my friends Ryan, John, Robert, Umesh, Nitin, Sarika, and Elliana.

My gratitude is also due to those who didn't play any direct role in publishing this book but extended their full support to make sure I was able to write this book. Thanks to my family.

Special thanks to my wife for helping me to make this possible.

About the Reviewers

Veerendra GG is a passionate Information Security researcher. He has been working in the Information Security domain for more than six years. His expertise includes vulnerability research, malware analysis, IDS/IPS signatures, exploit writing, and penetration testing. He has published a number of security advisories in a wide variety of applications and has also written Metasploit modules. He has been an active contributor to a number of open source applications that include OpenVAS, Snort, and Metasploit.

Currently, he works for SecPod Technologies Pvt Ltd as a Technical Lead and he has a Computer Science Engineering degree from Visvesvaraya Technological University, Belgaum, India.

> I would like to thank my friends, family, and the amazing people at SecPod for their unwavering support.

Martin MacLorrain Jr. has been a Navy Veteran for more than 10 years and has over 15 years' experience in Information Technology. His technical background includes Information Assurance Management, Vulnerability Assessment, Incident Response, Network Forensics, and Network Analysis, and he is fully qualified as DoD IAT/IAM/IASE level III. He is currently an independent consultant providing guidance to executive level personnel and also works in the trench training engineers and technicians for DoD, Federal Agencies, and Fortune 500 companies. When he spends time away from cyber security solutions architecture, he enjoys coaching in a youth football league and attending masonic functions. For more information about Martin, go to `martimac.info`.

> I would like to thank my good friend and great web developer 1dafo0L for keeping me motivated through out this process.

www.PacktPub.com

Support files, eBooks, discount offers and more

You might want to visit `www.PacktPub.com` for support files and downloads related to your book.

Did you know that Packt offers eBook versions of every book published, with PDF and ePub files available? You can upgrade to the eBook version at `www.PacktPub.com` and as a print book customer, you are entitled to a discount on the eBook copy. Get in touch with us at `service@packtpub.com` for more details.

At `www.PacktPub.com`, you can also read a collection of free technical articles, sign up for a range of free newsletters and receive exclusive discounts and offers on Packt books and eBooks.

`http://PacktLib.PacktPub.com`

Do you need instant solutions to your IT questions? PacktLib is Packt's online digital book library. Here, you can access, read and search across Packt's entire library of books.

Why Subscribe?

- Fully searchable across every book published by Packt
- Copy and paste, print and bookmark content
- On demand and accessible via web browser

Free Access for Packt account holders

If you have an account with Packt at `www.PacktPub.com`, you can use this to access PacktLib today and view nine entirely free books. Simply use your login credentials for immediate access.

Table of Contents

Preface

IT security is a vast and exciting domain, with Vulnerability Assessment and Penetration Testing as the most important and commonly performed activities across organizations to secure the IT infrastructure and to meet compliance requirements. *Learning Nessus for Penetration Testing* gives you an idea on how to perform VA and PT effectively using the commonly used tool named Nessus.

This book will introduce you to common tests such as Vulnerability Assessment and Penetration Testing. The introduction to the Nessus tool is followed by steps to install Nessus on Windows and Linux platforms. The book will explain step-by-step explain how to go about doing actual scanning and result interpretation, including further exploitation. Additional features offered such as using Nessus for compliance checks are also explained. Important concepts such as result analysis to remove false positives and criticality are also explained. How to go about performing Penetration Testing using the Nessus output is explained with the help of easy-to-understand examples. Finally, over the course of different chapters, tips and insights from real-world challenges faced during VA activity will be explained as well.

We hope you enjoy reading the book!

What this book covers

Chapter 1, Fundamentals, covers an introduction to Vulnerability Assessment and Penetration Testing, along with an introduction to Nessus as a tool and steps on installing and setting up Nessus.

Chapter 2, Scanning, explains how to configure a scan using Nessus. This chapter also covers the prerequisites for a scan, how to configure a scan policy, and so on.

Chapter 3, Scan Analysis, explains analysis of a scan's output, including result analysis, false positive analysis, vulnerability analysis, and exploiting vulnerabilities.

Chapter 4, *Reporting Options*, covers how to utilize different reporting options using Nessus. This chapter also talks about report generation, report customization, and report automation.

Chapter 5, *Compliance Checks*, explains how to utilize auditing options using Nessus, how it is different from Vulnerability Assessment, how an audit policy can be configured, and what the common compliance checks offered by Nessus for different environments are.

What you need for this book

It is assumed that you have a computer with the required configuration to install and run the Nessus tool. In order to run a sample scan, some authorized target machines of virtual images with different OSes will be useful.

Who this book is for

This book gives a good insight to security professionals, network administrators, network security professionals, security administrators, and information security officers on using Nessus's Vulnerability Scanner tool to conduct a Vulnerability Assessment to identify vulnerabilities in the IT infrastructure.

Conventions

In this book, you will find a number of styles of text that distinguish between different kinds of information. Here are some examples of these styles, and an explanation of their meaning.

Code words in text are shown as follows: "This option uses the `netstat` command available over the SSH connection to find open ports in a Unix system."

New terms and **important words** are shown in bold. Words that you see on the screen, in menus or dialog boxes for example, appear in the text like this: "Under the **Preferences** tab, there is a drop-down menu to choose different compliance checks."

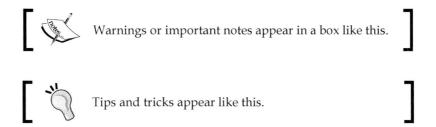

Warnings or important notes appear in a box like this.

Tips and tricks appear like this.

Reader feedback

Feedback from our readers is always welcome. Let us know what you think about this book—what you liked or may have disliked. Reader feedback is important for us to develop titles that you really get the most out of.

To send us general feedback, simply send an e-mail to `feedback@packtpub.com`, and mention the book title via the subject of your message.

If there is a topic that you have expertise in and you are interested in either writing or contributing to a book, see our author guide on `www.packtpub.com/authors`.

Customer support

Now that you are the proud owner of a Packt book, we have a number of things to help you to get the most from your purchase.

Errata

Although we have taken every care to ensure the accuracy of our content, mistakes do happen. If you find a mistake in one of our books—maybe a mistake in the text or the code—we would be grateful if you would report this to us. By doing so, you can save other readers from frustration and help us improve subsequent versions of this book. If you find any errata, please report them by visiting `http://www.packtpub.com/submit-errata`, selecting your book, clicking on the **errata submission form** link, and entering the details of your errata. Once your errata are verified, your submission will be accepted and the errata will be uploaded on our website, or added to any list of existing errata, under the Errata section of that title. Any existing errata can be viewed by selecting your title from `http://www.packtpub.com/support`.

Piracy

Piracy of copyright material on the Internet is an ongoing problem across all media. At Packt, we take the protection of our copyright and licenses very seriously. If you come across any illegal copies of our works, in any form, on the Internet, please provide us with the location address or website name immediately so that we can pursue a remedy.

Please contact us at `copyright@packtpub.com` with a link to the suspected pirated material.

We appreciate your help in protecting our authors, and our ability to bring you valuable content.

Questions

You can contact us at `questions@packtpub.com` if you are having a problem with any aspect of the book, and we will do our best to address it.

1
Fundamentals

These days, security is the most vital subject for any organization irrespective of their size or the kind of the business they do. The primary reason for this is that organizations don't want to lose their reputation or business over compromises affecting security; secondly, they have to meet legal and regulatory requirements. When it comes to technical security of the infrastructure, Vulnerability Assessment and Penetration Testing (PT or PenTest) play the most vital role. This chapter illustrates what a PT or PenTest is, why it is requiredand how to set up and manage Nessus for your organization.

This chapter will introduce you to Nessus, a tool for vulnerability assessment and penetration testing. We will also cover the following topics:

- Vulnerability Assessment
- Penetration testing
- Introduction to Nessus
- Installing Nessus on different platforms
- Updating Nessus plugins
- Nessus user management
- Nessus system configuration

Vulnerability Assessment and Penetration Testing

Vulnerability Assessment (VA) and **Penetrating Testing (PT or PenTest)** are the most common types of technical security risk assessments or technical audits conducted using different tools. These tools provide best outcomes if they are used optimally. An improper configuration may lead to multiple false positives that may or may not reflect true vulnerabilities. Vulnerability assessment tools are widely used by all, from small organizations to large enterprises, to assess their security status. This helps them with making timely decisions to protect themselves from these vulnerabilities. This book outlines the steps involved in conducting Vulnerability Assessments and PenTests using Nessus. Nessus is a widely recognized tool for such purposes. This section introduces you to basic terminology with reference to these two types of assessments.

Vulnerability in terms of IT systems can be defined as potential weaknesses in system/infrastructure that, if exploited, can result in the realization of an attack on the system.

An example of a vulnerability is a weak, dictionary-word password in a system that can be exploited by a brute force attack (dictionary attack) attempting to guess the password. This may result in the password being compromised and an unauthorized person gaining access to the system.

 The word **system** in this book refers to any asset existing in an information technology or non-information technology environment.

Vulnerability Assessment is a phase-wise approach to identifying the vulnerabilities existing in an infrastructure. This can be done using automated scanning tools such as Nessus, which uses its set of plugins corresponding to different types of known security loopholes in infrastructure, or a manual checklist-based approach that uses best practices and published vulnerabilities on well-known vulnerability tracking sites. The manual approach is not as comprehensive as a tool-based approach and will be more time-consuming. The kind of checks that are performed by a vulnerability assessment tool can also be done manually, but this will take a lot more time than an automated tool.

Penetration Testing has an additional step for vulnerability assessment, exploiting the vulnerabilities. Penetration Testing is an intrusive test, where the personnel doing the penetration test will first do a vulnerability assessment to identify the vulnerabilities, and as a next step, will try to penetrate the system by exploiting the identified vulnerabilities.

Need for Vulnerability Assessment

It is very important for you to understand why Vulnerability Assessment or Penetration Testing is required. Though there are multiple direct or indirect benefits for conducting a vulnerability assessment or a PenTest, a few of them have been recorded here for your understanding.

Risk prevention

Vulnerability Assessment uncovers the loopholes/gaps/vulnerabilities in the system. By running these scans on a periodic basis, an organization can identify known vulnerabilities in the IT infrastructure in time. Vulnerability Assessment reduces the likelihood of noncompliance to the different compliance and regulatory requirements since you know your vulnerabilities already. Awareness of such vulnerabilities in time can help an organization to fix them and mitigate the risks involved in advance before they get exploited. The risks of getting a vulnerability exploited include:

- Financial loss due to vulnerability exploits
- Organization reputation
- Data theft
- Confidentiality compromise
- Integrity compromise
- Availability compromise

Compliance requirements

The well-known information security standards (for example, ISO 27001, PCI DSS, and PA DSS) have control requirements that mandate that a Vulnerability Assessment must be performed.

A few countries have specific regulatory requirements for conducting Vulnerability Assessments in some specific industry sectors such as banking and telecom.

The life cycles of Vulnerability Assessment and Penetration Testing

This section describes the key phases in the life cycles of VA and PenTest. These life cycles are almost identical; Penetration Testing involves the additional step of exploiting the identified vulnerabilities.

It is recommended that you perform testing based on the requirements and business objectives of testing in an organization, be it Vulnerability Assessment or Penetration Testing. The following stages are involved in this life cycle:

1. Scoping
2. Information gathering
3. Vulnerability scanning
4. False positive analysis
5. Vulnerability exploitation (Penetration Testing)
6. Report generation

The following figure illustrates the different sequential stages recommended to follow for a Vulnerability Assessment or Penetration Testing:

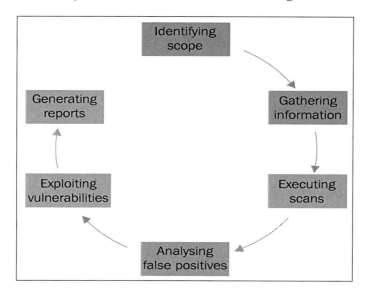

Stage 1 – scoping

Scoping is the primary step of any security assessment activity. In order to execute a VA or PenTest, the first step is to identify the scope of the assessment in terms of infrastructure against which the assessment is to be conducted, for example, servers, network devices, security devices, databases, and applications. Scoping depends on the business objective of the Vulnerability Assessment. During the scoping, a scanning window should also be agreed upon. Also, the types of attacks that are permitted should be agreed upon. After deciding on the scope of assessment, this phase also includes planning and preparation for the test, which includes deciding on the team, date, and time of the test. Another major factor that should be taken care of prior to beginning the engagement is signing a formal engagement agreement between the security tester and the party on whose infrastructure these tests will be performed. Scoping should also include identifying the count of infrastructure elements to be tested.

Apart from the infrastructure scope and other program management modalities, the exact scope, the organization's approach to the business objective, and the methodology of the assessment should be decided. For deciding on the business objective, the organization should identify the type of attack that it would like to get mimicked.

An example of an objective that a company might seek is: "To find out what an external attacker can achieve by targeting externally exposed infrastructure with only the knowledge of a publicaly exposed IP address." This type of requirement will be met through an external Blackbox penetration testing of infrastructure and applications, and the approach and the methodology should be in accordance with that.

Based on the accessibility of infrastructure from the Internet or intranet, the testing can be done from an external or internal network. Also, based on the type of details, the infrastructure testing can be Blackbox or Greybox. And depending on the type of infrastructure, the plugins or features of a vulnerability scanning tool should be enabled, aided by appropriate manual checks.

In Blackbox testing, only details such as the IP address are shared with the tester. Details giving an insight to the infrastructure, such as type and OS version, are not shared with respect to Nessus Scanner; this type of testing will involve a non credential scan (explained in *Chapter 2, Scanning*). This allows the tester to mimic an external attacker with limited knowledge about the infrastructure.

Greybox testing will include some details of the infrastructure to be shared, such as the type of device and software version that allow getting more comprehensive and administrator credentials fed to the tool for more comprehensive results. In addition, to mimic an internal attacker with knowledge about the infrastructure with respect to Nessus Scanner, this type of testing will involve credentialed scanning, giving more comprehensive results.

Stage 2 – information gathering

Information gathering is the second and most important stage of a VA-PT assessment. This stage includes finding out information about the target system using both technical (WhoIS) and nontechnical passive methods such as the search engine and Internet groups). This step is critical as it helps in getting a better picture of the target infrastructure and its resources. As the timeline of the assessment is generally time bound, information captured during this phase helps in streamlining the effort of testing in the right direction by using the right tools and approach applicable to target systems. This step becomes more important for a Blackbox assessment where very limited information about the target system is shared.

Information gathering is followed by a more technical approach to map the target network using utilities such as pings and Telnet and using port scanners such as NMAP. The use of such tools would enable assessors to find a live host, open services, operating systems, and other information.

The information gathered through network mapping will further validate information gathered through other passive means about the target infrastructure, which is important to configure the vulnerability scanning tool. This ensures that scanning is done more appropriately.

Stage 3 – vulnerability scanning

This stage involves the actual scanning of the target infrastructure to identify existing vulnerabilities of the system. This is done using vulnerability scanners such as Nessus. Prior to scanning, the tool should be configured optimally as per the target infrastructure information captured during the initial phases. Care should also be taken that the tool is able to reach the target infrastructure by allowing access through relevant intermediate systems such as firewalls. Such scanners perform protocol TCP, UDP, and ICMP scans to find open ports and services running on the target machine and match them to well-known published vulnerabilities updated regularly in the tool's signature database if they exist in the target infrastructure. The output of this phase gives an overall view of what kind of vulnerabilities exist in the target infrastructure that if exploited can lead to system compromise.

Stage 4 – false positive analysis

As an output of the scanning phase, one would obtain a list of vulnerabilities of the target infrastructure. One of the key activities to be performed with the output would be false positive analysis, that is, removing any vulnerability that is falsely reported by the tool and does not exist in reality. All scanning tools are prone to report false positives, and this analysis can be done using methods such as correlating vulnerabilities with each other and previously gathered information and scan reports, along with actually checking whether system access is available.

Vulnerability scanners give their own risk rating to the identified vulnerabilities; these can be revisited considering the actual criticality of the infrastructure element (server or network device) to the network and impact of the vulnerability.

Stage 5 – vulnerability exploitation (Penetration Testing)

In case system owners require proof of existing vulnerabilities or exploits to understand the extent to which an attacker can compromise a vulnerable system, testers will be required to demonstrate exploits in a controlled environment with out actually making the infrastructure unavailable, unless that's a requirement. Penetration Testing is the next step to Vulnerability Assessment aiming to penetrate the target system based on exploits available for the identified vulnerabilities. For exploitation, our own knowledge or publicaly available exploits of well-known vulnerabilities can be utilized. Penetration Testing or Vulnerability Exploitation can be broadly divided into phases such as preexploitation, exploitation, and postexploitation.

Activities in the pre-exploitation phase are explained in phases 1 to 4, that is, enumerating the infrastructure and identifying the vulnerability.

Once any vulnerability is exploited to gain access to the system, the attacker should aim to further detail the network by sniffing traffic, mapping the internal network, and trying to obtain a higher privilege account to gain the maximum level of access to the system. This will enable testers to launch further attacks on the network to further increase the scope of compromised systems. The postexploitation step will also involve clearing of tracks by conducting activities such as clearing logs and disabling antivirus.

As a post-exploitation phase tester, you can demonstrate how an attacker can maintain access to the system through backdoors and rootkits.

Stage 6 – report generation

After completing the assessment as per the scope of work, final reporting needs to be done covering the following key areas:

- A brief introduction about the assessment

- The scope of assessment

- The management/executive summary

- A synopsis of findings with risk severity

- Details about each finding with their impact and your recommendations to fix the vulnerability

Introduction to Nessus

Nessus is one of the most widely-used Vulnerability Assessment products. First released in the year 1998 by *Renaud Deraison*, this tool has been one of the most popular vulnerability scanning tools used across the industry for the past 15 years.

The official website of Nessus (`http://www.tenable.com`) describes it as follows:

> *"Nessus® is the industry's most widely-deployed vulnerability and configuration assessment product. Nessus features high-speed discovery, configuration auditing, asset profiling, sensitive data discovery, patch management integration, and vulnerability analysis of your security posture. Fueled by Nessus ProfessionalFeed®, a continuously-updated library with more than 50,000 individual vulnerability and configuration checks, and supported by an expert vulnerability research team, Nessus delivers accuracy to the marketplace. Nessus scales to serve the largest organizations and is quick-and-easy to deploy."*

Over the years, Nessus has evolved from a pure play vulnerability scanner to include added assessment and auditing features such as configuration auditing, compliance auditing, patch auditing, control system auditing, and mobile device auditing. It is best known for the ease and flexibility offered by its Vulnerability Assessment feature.

The key infrastructure that is covered under Nessus Vulnerability Scanner includes the following:

- **Network devices**: These include Juniper, Cisco, firewalls, and printers
- **Virtual hosts**: These include VMware ESX, ESXi, vSphere, and vCenter
- **Operating systems**: These include Windows, Mac, Linux, Solaris, BSD, Cisco iOS, and IBM iSeries
- **Databases**: These include Oracle, MS SQL Server, MySQL, DB2, Informix/ DRDA, and PostgreSQL
- **Web applications**: These include web servers, web services, and OWASP vulnerabilities

Nessus Vulnerability Scanner is an easy-to-use tool. Someone new to the tool can learn it easily.

Initial Nessus setup

The detailed steps on how to install Nessus have been given later in this chapter. Once you install Nessus, you can do one-time setups for your Nessus scanner such as setting up user accounts to access the scanner; general settings, such as configuring SMTP or a web proxy, feed settings, mobile settings, and result settings; and configuring advanced configuration settings. These settings have been detailed later in this chapter. They are very unique to your scanning environment, which depends on your organization's security policies and preferences. You may also want to create some generic policies before you go for the scan, depending on the requirements.

Scheduling scans

Nessus provides the flexibility to schedule scans on target hosts for future scanning. This is as good as job scheduling. You can configure and schedule in advance with a predefined time and policy. Nessus will automatically initiate the scan at the defined time and e-mail the results to predefined e-mail IDs. This doesn't need any manual trigger to invoke scans. You can also schedule repeat scans such as "my scan target IPs should be scanned every Thursday at 3 AM CET". Most of the time, large enterprise organizations face a lot of challenges to identifying a scanning window. A scanning window is a time frame for the scan that defines at what time the scan should take place and the time by when the scan should be completed.

Usually, the scanning window is decided based on the production load on the scanning machines. It is recommended that production machines be scanned only in nonpeak hours. Nonpeak hours is the time when the target or scanning machine is least used during a day/week.

The Nessus plugin

To enable a comprehensive coverage of security checks, Nessus provides a large variety of plugins grouped together to provide similar security checks. Grouping allows disabling or enabling a large quantity of plugins based on target machines in one go. Examples of the major plugin family include Windows, Linux, Solaris, Cisco, and Database. For details about plugins and the difference between the home feed and professional feed families, please refer to the Nessus official website at `https://plugins.nessus.org`.

Nessus, being one of the most widely-used tools, has an active online support community at `https://discussions.nessus.org`.

Nessus is one of the most cost-efficient scanning tools available with features such as low total cost of ownership (TCO) and scan unlimited number of IPs. Nessus subscriptions include software updates, access to Tenable's compliance and audit files, and support. Additionally, it also includes the daily update of vulnerability and configuration checks with automated installation.

 Apart from introducing Nessus, this chapter describes the basics of Vulnerability Assessment and Penetration Testing, two of the most common types of technical risk assessment conducted using Nessus. Along with this, various installation options in Nessus are also described.

Patch management using Nessus

Nessus is very successful in patch management; this is achieved by integrating Nessus with a variety of patch management solutions. The good part here is that you need not supply credentials to Nessus for scanning the target machines; instead, you need to supply the credentials for the patch management system. This is because the patch management system will already have the credentials to reach the target host.

Governance, risk, and compliance checks using Nessus

Nessus provides outputs in different formats, such as HTML, CSV, and PDF. This makes it much more flexible to feed the output to different tools to integrate with. These tools can be governance, risk, and compliance tools such as EMC RSA Archer SmartSuit or any other similar tool.

Installing Nessus on different platforms

Nessus supports almost all the popular operating systems. Depending on the availability of the operating system, the required installation steps given in this section can be followed to install Nessus. The latest information/steps can also be fetched from Nessus's official website. At the time of writing this book, Nessus supports the following operating system platforms:

- Microsoft Windows – XP, 2003, 2008, Vista, 2012, 7, and 8
- Linux – Debian, Red Hat, Fedora, SuSE, Ubuntu
- Solaris
- Mac
- Free BSD
- Checksums and GCP keys

The latest details about the preceding list can be obtained from Tenable Nessus's official website at `http://www.tenable.com/`.

Prerequisites

The scanning machine should have 4 GB of memory (preferably). However, refer to Nessus's official website `http://www.tenable.com/` for the latest requirements.

A better processor will support facilitating a fast scan. The scanning machine should be selected by keeping the scope of the Nessus scan in view; if you plan to do a vulnerability assessment for a big enterprise, it is recommended that a high-end server machine be used.

 No firewall should block the traffic generated by Nessus to reach scanning target systems. If a firewall is in place, a firewall rule should be configured to allow all the traffic generated by the Nessus machine to reach scanning targets. Please don't forget to deactivate this firewall rule once the scan activity is completed.

If you reach out to scanning machines using a web proxy, proxy authentication credentials should be keyed in Nessus. This is an optional setting depending on your scanning environment.

You should have administrative rights on the machine to install Nessus, and the Nessus plugin feed activation code is required to update plugins.

Installing Nessus on Windows 7

For the latest Nessus package, either to buy or to evaluate, you should browse through to Tenable Nessus's official website at `http://www.tenable.com/`:

1. Log in to the Nessus website to buy and download the latest Nessus software from the **Products** section.

    The Nessus software package should be downloaded according to the operating system you want to install Nessus for. The steps given on Nessus's website should be followed for downloading the Nessus package.

    It is important to note that Nessus should be downloaded as per the scanning machine operating system from which you plan to scan other systems, not by the operating systems which you are going to scan. For example, if you need to scan 10 Linux machines, one Solaris machine, and five Windows machines from a Windows 2008 server machine, download the Nessus package for the Windows 2008 operating system. Depending on the bit count of the operation system, you may choose a 32-bit/64-bit package.

2. Once you have downloaded the Nessus executable file (the Nessus setup package), double-click on it to begin the installation. In case you don't have administrative privileges, press *Shift* and right-click on the executable file; click on **Run as** to run the installer with an administrative account.

3. You might receive a security warning **Do you want to run this file?**. Click on the **Run** button.

4. After clicking on **Run**, the installer will pop up a window to proceed with the installation.

5. Click on **Next**, and this will pop up the window with the Nessus license agreement. It is very important for everyone to read through the license agreement and abide by the same.

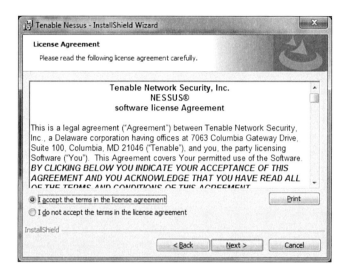

6. To proceed further with the Nessus installation, you need to accept the license agreement and click on **Next**.

7. You have an option to change the directory where you want to install Nessus. Click on **Next** to proceed further.

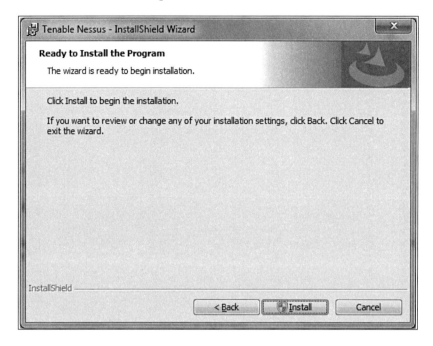

8. Click on **Install** to proceed further.

9. During the installation, you might get one more prompt saying **Would you like to install this device software?**. Select the checkbox **Always trust software from Tenable network security Inc.** if you need to trust all software from Tenable. This option is not mandatory to select. Click on **Install** on this security window pop up to proceed further.

10. The following screenshot indicates successful installation. Click on **Finish** to proceed further:

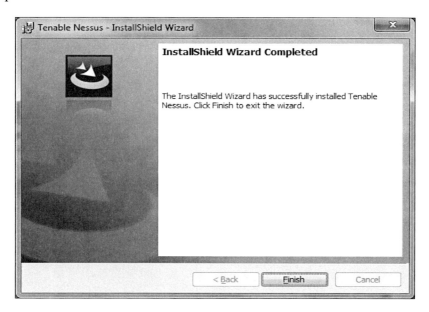

Post successful Nessus installation, it takes you to basic configurations such as default settings, user creations, and activation code.

The following screenshot shows the web view of the Nessus installed. Nessus runs on port 8834 by default:

Welcome to Nessus!

Please connect via SSL by clicking here.

You are likely to get a security alert from your web browser saying that the SSL certificate is invalid. You may either choose to temporarily accept the risk, or you can obtain a valid SSL certificate from a registrar. Please refer to the Nessus documentation for more information.

Nessus warns about the SSL certificate. It doesn't come with an SSL certificate by default. Nessus administrators have to get an SSL certificate to configure Nessus with SSL.

If you want to install an SSL certificate now itself, install it; otherwise, click on **Proceed anyway**. This will take you to the kind of introduction page to begin with.

Click on **Get Started** to proceed further.

Welcome to Nessus® 5

Thank you for installing Nessus, the world leader in vulnerability scanners. Nessus will allow you to perform:

- High-speed vulnerability discovery, to determine which hosts are running which services
- Agentless auditing, to make sure no host on your network is missing security patches
- Compliance checks, to verify and prove that every host on your network adheres to the security policy you defined
- Scan scheduling, to automatically run scans at the frequency you select
- And more!

During the next steps, we are going to create an administrative account and register your scanner with a Plugin Feed, which we will download. You will need an Activation Code before you can use Nessus; if you do not have an Activation Code already, please go to http://www.nessus.org/register/ to get one now.

Get started >

The first thing you need to do after this is the administrative account setup. This account is created on the Nessus server. This account should always be remembered for Nessus administration.

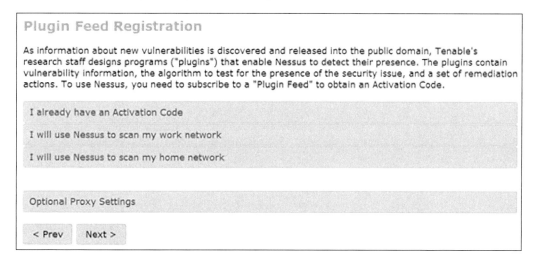

After the administrative account creation, Nessus will prompt for plugin feed registration and proxy settings, which is optional.

Plugin feed registration has to be done as per your anticipated use. After registration, you get an activation code that you need to use for plugin subscription.

Installing Nessus on Linux

For the latest Nessus package, either for buying or evaluation purposes, you should visit Tenable Nessus's official website at `http://www.tenable.com/`:

1. Log in to the Nessus website to buy and download the latest Nessus software from the **Products** section as per your operating system and version. The steps outlined here are for Red Hat Linux 5.2.

2. Once you have downloaded the Nessus executable file (the Nessus setup package), double-click on it to start the installation procedure. Administrative/root rights are required for installation.

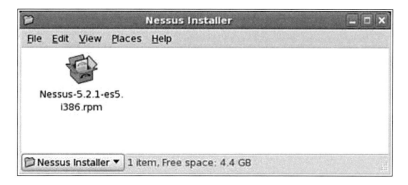

You will see the **Installing packages** window shown in the following screenshot:

3.   Click on the **Apply** button.

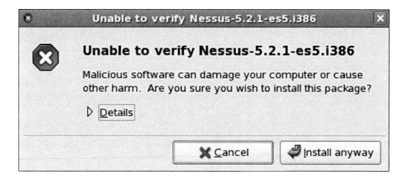

4.   Click on **Install anyway** to proceed further with the installation.

The preceding screenshot shows that Nessus is installed successfully on the Red Hat Linux environment. To begin with this, the Nessus service should be started.

5. The following command should be executed to start the Nessus service on the Linux terminal:

```
# /sbin/service nessusd start
```

The following screenshot shows the Nessus service starting up with the status **OK**:

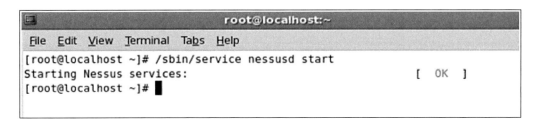

6. To configure the Nessus scanner, type the URL `https://localhost.localdomain:8834/` into the Linux box web browser.

This page displays the secure connection error, which can be rectified by adding an exception to the web browser.

7. Click on the **Or you can add an exception** link.

8. Click on **Add Exception** and on **Get Certificate**. This will activate the button **Confirm Security Exception**. Once you click on this , the web browser will display the Nessus scanner home page.

To configure further, the same steps as outlined for the Windows installation can be followed for registration, activation, updating plugins, user management, and so on.

Definition update

Updating Nessus definitions (plugins) is important as this keeps Nessus updated and able to identify all the latest vulnerabilities. To conduct a successful vulnerability scan with Nessus, it is important to check and update Nessus with the latest plugins before conducting scans.

To update Nessus on a Windows machine, the following steps should be performed:

1. Log in to the Nessus server with the administrator account.

2. Click on the **Configuration** tab from the top menu bar.

3. After clicking on the **Configuration** tab, Nessus will open up the system configuration settings. This will have subtabs, namely **General Settings**, **Feed Settings**, **Mobile Settings**, **Results Settings**, and **Advanced Settings**.

4. Click on the **Feed Settings** tab on the left-hand selection panel. This will open up a page to update the Nessus plugins feed.

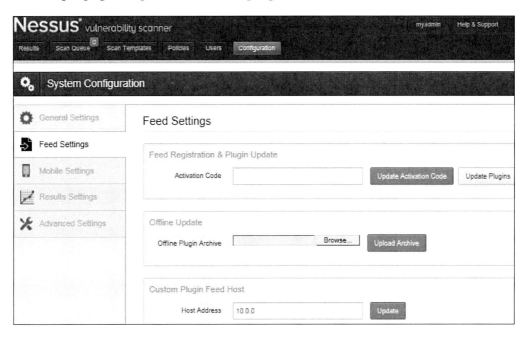

Nessus provides multiple feed options as follows:

- Online plugin updates
- Offline plugin updates
- Custom plugins feed host-based updates

Online plugin updates

Online plugin update is the most popular option for updating Nessus plugins and provides the ability to update the plugins through the Internet. This requires an Internet connection of fairly good speed on the Nessus machine. After Nessus registration and activation, plugins can be updated by clicking on the **Update Plugins** button.

Offline plugin updates

Offline plugin update is used when plugins are archived in a local directory from where Nessus can take the feed and update. This doesn't need an Internet connection on the Nessus system. To set up an offline update, first get the Nessus subscription activation code, which can be retrieved from Nessus support or the registered e-mail ID used for Nessus feed registration.

The next step is to generate a challenge code that is used to download plugins along with the activation code.

To generate the challenge code on a Windows Nessus machine, run the following command in the command-line tool:

```
\Program Files\Tenable\Nessus> nessus-fetch.exe --challenge
```

For a Linux Nessus machine, the command is slightly different; the following command should be run on a Linux terminal:

```
# /opt/nessus/bin/nessus-fetch --challenge
```

This will generate a long string of characters, which is called a challenge code. An example challenge code is `19c4ed603ac3e436a14239852c8fbf8f26f02d7b`.

In order to continue downloading plugins offline, go to the Nessus plugins offline download page at `https://plugins.nessus.org/offline.php`. Once loaded, the page prompts for the challenge code and activation code. Enter these in.

Custom plugins feed host-based updates

A custom plugins feed host can be set up using this option. The hostname or host IP address can be provided to set this up.

User management

User management is an additional feature provided by Nessus that is most useful for a large enterprise environment where Nessus is used by multiple people in multiple locations. In such an environment, this feature enables administrators to enable different levels of access for multiple users on the Nessus scanner.

Nessus provides two different roles for users as follows:

- Administrator
- Nonadministrator

An administrator role has access to all functionalities of Nessus, whereas a non-administrator role has limited access. The non-administrator role doesn't have access to user management, general settings, feed settings, and advanced settings.

While installing Nessus, an administrative user is created for Nessus administration. To proceed with Nessus user management, it is necessary to log in with this account as it has administrator privileges.

The URL `https://localhost:8834/` can be browsed to on a Windows machine.

Enter the administrator username and password to sign in. This displays the home page of Nessus as shown in the preceding screenshot.

Multiple tabs will be displayed under the administrative login. Click on the **Users** tab to move further with user management activities.

In Nessus, user management provides the following options:

- Adding a new user
- Deleting an existing user
- Changing the password for an existing user
- Changing the role of an existing user

Adding a new user

Click on the **New User** button to add a new user.

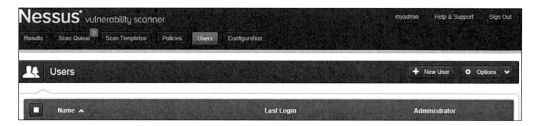

This will display the new user prompt to set the username, password, and role for the new user as shown in the following screenshot:

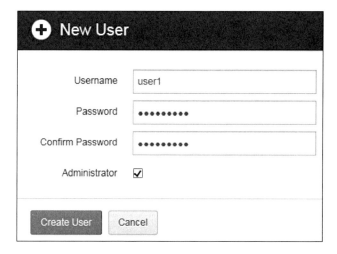

Deleting an existing user

Delete User is a functionality used when a user is no longer required on the Nessus scanner. In such cases, select the user who needs to be deleted from the **Users** header and click on the **Delete User** button from the options displayed on the right-hand side.

Changing the password or role of an existing user

At times, an administrator receives requests to change passwords for users. It may be because a user has forgotten his/her password or because his/her role needs to be changed. In such cases, select the user for whom the password or role needs to be changed and double-click on that user. This will prompt you with the following window for a new password to be set or the role to be changed:

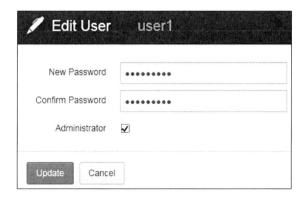

Nessus system configuration

Nessus system configuration settings can be referred to under the **Configuration** tab. This has five different groups of settings as follows:

- General Settings
- Feed Settings
- Mobile Settings
- Result Settings
- Advanced Settings

General Settings

The **General Settings** tab can be seen under **Configuration** by logging in to Nessus with administrator privileges. There are two different options of **General Settings** that exist in the **Setting Type** dropdown:

- SMTP Server
- Web Proxy

The SMTP server settings allow you to configure the SMTP server with your Nessus server to send out results of completed scans by automated e-mails.

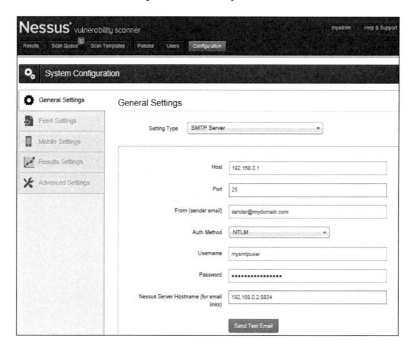

SMTP settings

Different settings for SMTP can be configured as per your SMTP configuration. SMTP settings are explained in the following table:

SMTP setting	Description
Host	The SMTP server hostname or IP.
Port	The port number to connect the SMTP server.
From (Sender email)	E-mail ID from the report e-mails should appear as a sender.
Auth Method	The SMTP authentication method.
Username	The username with which to authenticate to the SMTP server.
Password	The password corresponding with this username.
Nessus Server Hostname	This is only for the e-mail links, Nessus server hostname, or IP address to be specified.
Send Test Email	Lets you test by sending a test e-mail.

Web proxy settings

Some organizations host a web proxy server between the external and internal networks to pass the traffic through. To update Nessus with the latest plugins in a web proxy environment, it is necessary to configure web proxy settings as per organization setup. This enables Nessus to reach the Nessus plugin server over the Internet to download the latest plugins.

Different settings for the web proxy can be configured as per your web proxy configuration. These settings are explained in the following table:

Web proxy setting	Description
Host	The proxy hostname or IP.
Port	The port number for the proxy to connect.
Username	The username to connect the proxy to.
Password	The password for the username to connect the proxy to.
User-agent	Required if the proxy uses filter-specific HTTP user agents. The custom user agent string needs to be specified.

Feed Settings

Feed Settings is explained in the *Definition update* section in this chapter.

Mobile Settings

The issue of mobile device security has become the priority in recent times with the widespread use of mobile devices in the corporate domain with concepts such as **Bring Your Own Device** (**BYOD**) being used proactively. Such devices when connected to corporate networks bring with them the inherent vulnerabilities of their mobile platforms. Nessus offers a mobile security scanning option where information and vulnerabilities for mobile devices recently connected to respective servers are scanned.

Currently, plugins related to the iPhone 4, the iPad, Windows Phone, and Android devices are included, and Nessus has the ability to scan **Active Directory Service Interfaces** (**ADSI**) and Apple Profile Manager to identify mobile devices connected to these servers, and to identify vulnerabilities.

The **Mobile Settings** tab presents options to configure the settings for the following type:

- **ActiveSync (Exchange)**
- **Apple Profile Manager**
- **Good For Enterprise**

This can be seen in the following screenshot:

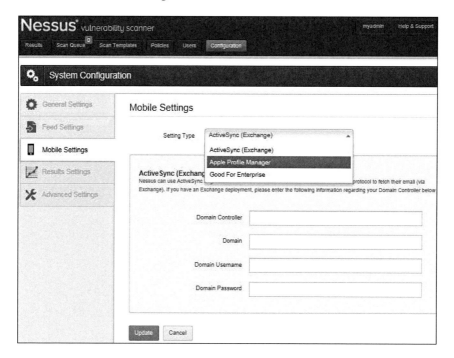

ActiveSync (Exchange)

Nessus can be configured to use ActiveSync for gathering information about all the mobile devices that use this protocol to fetch their e-mail (via Exchange). If you have an Exchange deployment, you can configure the domain controller settings, as listed in the following table:

ActiveSync mobile setting	Description
Domain Controller	The domain controller IP.
Domain	The domain name.
Domain Username	The username to connect the domain to.
Domain Password	The password for the username to connect to.

Apple Profile Manager

Nessus can be configured to use Apple Profile Manager for gathering information about all the iOS devices. If you have Apple Profile Manager deployed, you can configure the Apple Profile Manager settings, as listed in the following table:

Apple Profile Manager mobile setting	Description
Apple Profile Manager server	The Apple Profile Manager server IP.
Apple Profile Manager port	The Apple Profile Manager server port to connect to.
Apple Profile Manager username	The username to log in with.
Apple Profile Manager password	The password that corresponds with the username.
SSL	Check/uncheck this option based on the environment.
Verify SSL Certificate	Check this option if you want the SSL certificate to be verified.
Force Device Updates	Check this option if you want a device update to be forced.
Device Update Timeout (Minutes)	The device update timeout in minutes.

Good For Enterprise

Nessus can be configured to use Good Mobile device management for gathering information about all the mobile devices that use this protocol. If you have Good For Enterprise deployed, you can configure the settings listed in the following table:

Good For Enterprise mobile setting	Description
GMC Server	The GMC server IP needs to be mentioned here.
Port	The port number to use to connect with the GMC server.
Domain	The domain name.
Username	The username to connect with.
Password	The password that corresponds with the username.
SSL	Check/uncheck this option based on the environment.
Verify SSL Certificate	Check this option if you want a device to be verified.

Result Settings

Result Settings can be seen under **Configurations**. This allows you to add rules to disable plugins or change their severity.

The following screenshot shows how to add a new plugin rule:

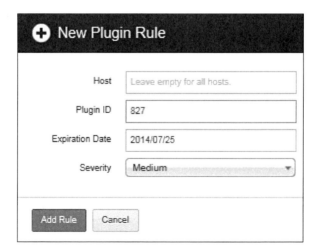

The following table illustrates the new plugin rule options in detail:

New plugin rule option	Description
Host	If the result plugin rule is only for a particular IP/host, the host can be mentioned in the Host field. If the rule is to be applied for the entire host scanned, this can be left blank.
Plugin ID	The plugin ID to be provided to specify which plugin the rule is for.
Expiration Date	The expiration date for a rule can be specified here in case it needs to expire on a particular date.
Severity	Severity can be set from the dropdown as per the rule you want to set. It may be Hidden, Informational, Low, Medium, High, or Critical.

Advanced Settings

The Nessus GUI configuration menu contains several configurable options.

It is recommended that these settings be reviewed and modified appropriately based on your scanning environment. The option can be changed and saved using the **Save** button or can be removed altogether using the **X** sign present next to the option.

Special care should be taken while modifying the `max_hosts` and `max_checks` values in the upcoming table. These values represent the maximum number of checks and hosts being scanned at one time and have a direct impact on the scanning to be performed. The `max_checks` value, if greater than **5**, can have an adverse impact on target servers, so it should be avoided. Similarly, a high value of `max_hosts` can overwhelm the host scanning system, and it depends on the capacity of the host on which Nessus is installed. It is recommended that this value also be kept relatively low (can start with 10); it can be optimized as per the environment and system capability.

The following screenshot shows some of the options from the table following it; options can be added or removed using the **Add Settings** tab and the **X** button respectively.

The advanced setting options and their uses as per the Nessus documentation are mentioned in the following table:

New plugin rule options	Description	The default value
allow_post_scan_editing	If enabled, post scan editing is possible.	**Yes**
auto_enable_ dependencies	Automatically activates the plugins that depend on it. If disabled, not all plugins may run despite being selected in the scan policy.	**Yes**
auto_update	Controls automatic plugin updates. If enabled and Nessus is registered, it fetches the newest plugins from plugins. nessus.org automatically. Disable if the scanner is on an isolated network not able to reach the Internet.	**Yes**
auto_update_delay	The number of hours to wait between two updates. Four hours (4) is the minimum allowed interval.	**24**
cgi_path	During the testing of web servers, use the colon-delimited list of CGI paths.	`/cgi-bin:/ scripts`
checks_read_timeout	Lets you specify the read timeout for the sockets of the tests.	**5**
disable_ntp	Disables the old NTP legacy protocol.	**Yes**
disable_xmlrpc	Disables the new XMLRPC (web server) interface.	**No**
Dumpfile	Lets you specify the location of a dump file for debugging output if generated.	`C:\ ProgramData\ Tenable\ Nessus\nessus\ logs\nessusd. dump`
global.max_hosts	The maximum number of hosts that can be scanned.	**130**
global.max_scans	If set to nonzero, this allows you to define the maximum number of scans that may take place in parallel.	**0**
global.max_simult_tcp_ sessions	The maximum number of simultaneous TCP connections	**50**
global.max_web_users	If set to nonzero, this defines the maximum of (web) users that can connect in parallel.	**1024**

New plugin rule options	Description	The default value
listen_address	The IPv4 address to listen for incoming connections. If set to 127.0.0.1, this will restrict access to local connections only.	**0.0.0.0**
listen_port	The port to listen for (the old NTP protocol). Used for pre-4.2 NessusClient connections.	**1241**
log_whole_attack	Allows you to log every detail of the attack and is helpful for debugging issues with the scan, but this may be disk intensive.	**No**
Logfile	Where the Nessus logfile is stored.	`C:\ ProgramData\ Tenable\ Nessus\nessus\ logs\nessusd. messages`
max_checks	The maximum number of simultaneous checks against each host tested.	**5**
max_hosts	The maximum number of hosts checked at one time during a scan.	**5**
nasl_log_type	Direct the type of NASL engine output in `nessusd.dump`.	**Normal**
nasl_no_signature_check	Allows you to specify whether Nessus should consider all NASL scripts as being signed. Selecting Yes is unsafe and is not recommended.	**No**
non_simult_ports	Lets you speficy those ports against which two plugins should not be run simultaneously.	**139, 445, 3389**
optimize_test	Lets you optimize the test procedure. Changing this to No will cause scans to take longer and typically generate more false positives.	**Yes**
plugin_upload	Lets you designate whether administrator users may upload plugins.	**Yes**
plugins_timeout	The maximum lifetime of a plugin's activity (in seconds).	**320**
port_range	The range of ports the port scanners will scan. Can use the keywords the **Default** or **All** as well as a comma-delimited list of ports or ranges of ports.	**Default**

New plugin rule options	Description	The default value
purge_plugin_db	Lets you specify whether Nessus should purge the plugin database at each update. This directs Nessus to remove, redownload, and rebuild the plugin database for each update. Choosing **Yes** will cause each update to be considerably slower.	**No**
qdb_mem_usage	Directs Nessus to use more or less memory when idle. If Nessus is running on a dedicated server, setting this to **High** will use more memory to increase performance. If Nessus is running on a shared machine, setting this to **Low** will use considerably less memory, but at the price of a moderate performance impact.	**Low**
reduce_connections_on_congestion	Lets you reduce connections in case of congestion.	**No**
report_crashes	Allows you to specify whether to anonymously report crashes to Tenable.	**Yes**
Rules	The location of the Nessus rules file (nessusd.rules).	`C:\ ProgramData\ Tenable\ Nessus\conf\ nessusd.rules`
safe_checks	Safe checks rely on banner grabbing rather than active testing for a vulnerability.	**Yes**
silent_dependencies	If this is enabled, the list of plugin dependencies and their outputs are not included in the report. A plugin may be selected as part of a policy that depends on other plugins to run. By default, Nessus will run those plugin dependencies but will not include their outputs in the report. Setting this option to **No** will cause both the selected plugin and any plugin dependencies to appear in the report.	**Yes**

New plugin rule options	Description	The default value
slice_network_ addresses	If this option is set, Nessus will not scan a network incrementally (10.0.0.1, then 10.0.0.2, then 10.0.0.3, and so on) but will attempt to slice the workload throughout the whole network (for examaple, it will scan 10.0.0.1, then 10.0.0.127, then 10.0.0.2, then 10.0.0.128, and so on).	No
ssl_cipher_list	Makes sure that only "strong" SSL ciphers are used while connecting to port 1241. Supports the keyword strong or the general OpenSSL designations as listed at http://www.openssl.org/docs/apps/ciphers.html.	Strong
stop_scan_on_ disconnect	Lets you stop scanning a host that seems to have been disconnected during the scan.	No
stop_scan_on_hang	Lets you stop a scan that seems to be hung up.	No
throttle_scan	The throttle scan is for when the CPU is overloaded.	Yes
www_logfile	Lets you specify where the Nessus web server (user interface) log is stored.	C:\ ProgramData\ Tenable\ Nessus\nessus\ logs\www_ server.log
xmlrpc_idle_ session_timeout	The idle session timeout for Nessus.	30
xmlrpc_listen_port	The port for the Nessus web server to listen for (the new XMLRPC protocol).	8834

All these advanced settings need to be analyzed properly before being applied. The recommended settings may vary from environment to environment.

A few sections of this chapter, which are specific configuration settings, have been referenced from learning material available on Nessus website: http://www.tenable.com.

Summary

In this chapter, we learned the basics about Vulnerability Assessment and Penetration Testing as well as had an introduction to Nessus.

VA and PT are key types of technical risk assessment, where VA concentrates on finding weaknesses or vulnerabilities in the infrastructure and PT goes to the next level to exploit these vulnerabilities.

Such assessments are carried out as preventive control to identify and mitigate vulnerabilities or out of various compliance requirements. Key activities for such tests include scoping, information gathering, vulnerability scanning, false positive analysis, vulnerability exploitation (Penetration Testing), and report generation. Scoping includes a different approach to testing Blackbox (no information about infrastructure) and Greybox (credentials and details about infrastructure are shared).

In this chapter, we also got an introduction to Nessus as one of the widely-used vulnerability scanners. It uses security checks, called plugins, against which vulnerabilities are identified during a scan. The key plugin family includes Windows, Linux, Solaris, Cisco, and Databases. Over the years, Nessus has added features such as configuration and compliance checks, apart from the primary functionality of the vulnerability scanner.

Nessus can be installed on all the major operating systems and detailed steps for installing Nessus on Windows 7 and Linux OS—along with the prerequisites—are mentioned in this chapter.

During initial setup, the initial administrator account is created to log in to Nessus as the administrator, and based on the requirement, the home or professional feed is activated.

This is followed by updating the plugin. The option to update plugins offline is also explained. Nessus offers a user management section to create Nessus users and grant those privileges for future use. Finally, Nessus system configuration settings such as **Feed Settings**, **Mobile Settings**, and **Advanced Settings** were introduced.

In the next chapter, we will learn about scanning the IT infrastructure using Nessus.

2
Scanning

Vulnerability scanning, or in other terms, identification of vulnerabilities in the target infrastructure, is the key activity performed by any vulnerability scanner such as Nessus. While using such scanners to perform a Vulnerability Assessment, it is of prime importance to configure the scan parameter, in the most efficient way, keeping the target infrastructure in mind. This will result in getting the most effective scan results in the optimized scan time.

This chapter will introduce how to set up Nessus for vulnerability scanning. Scan configuration in Nessus involves two major steps, namely configuration of a scan policy and launching a scan using the configured policy. The key areas that will be covered in this chapter are as follows:

- Scan prerequisites
- Policy configuration
- Credential and noncredential scan
- Scan configuration
- Scan execution and results

Scan prerequisites

A successful vulnerability scan requires a proper setup of Nessus with certain prerequisites. This will make sure that all approvals are documented, all backups are in place, and the scanning windows have been agreed before you scan. Nessus cannot reach the target with a firewall in between that is blocking the traffic/packets.

We will now see the most common prerequisites, which are applicable to most of the Nessus scans; however, I encourage you to be analyzing as per your scanning environment and the organization's applicability.

Scan-based target system admin credentials

It is always recommended to run with a credentials scan for better results; this means that before you scan a target system, you should obtain the target system's credentials or have someone who can key-in the target system administrative credentials in the Nessus GUI without sharing with you before you start the scan. This will help Nessus to probe the target system more and more to uncover maximum vulnerabilities. If you are performing a Blackbox scan where you will not have access to the credentials, this particular prerequisite stands inapplicable.

Direct connectivity without a firewall

It is recommended to have direct connectivity of Nessus with the target systems for better results; this means there should not be a firewall or any other device blocking traffic in between of Nessus and the target systems. If a firewall is in between of Nessus and the target systems, a firewall rule should be configured to allow all traffic in between of Nessus and the target systems. Don't forget to remove or deactivate this rule immediately after scan completion. This is required because Nessus generates a lot of malicious packets/traffic to the target systems for probing the vulnerabilities. In case a firewall is in place, this will drop all such malicious packets from reaching the target system.

Scanning window to be agreed upon

It is the owner of the target system who can let you know the best suitable time for the vulnerability scan depending on the peak and off-peak load on the target systems. This suitable time window is called the **scanning window**. If you are running a scan on the production systems, it is very important to agree on a scanning window, preferably with the target system owners. It is recommended to run Nessus scans during off-peak hours when the target system has minimum load.

Scanning approvals and related paper work

It is important to have a clear discussion with the target system owners to make them understand the impacts, which might take place due to a malicious scan, which may or may not be an intrusive scan. Each party should understand the risk of carrying out vulnerability scans and agree to it. This should be documented for legal purposes. Also, a non-disclosure agreement should be duly signed by each person of the team conducting the Vulnerability Assessment or Penetration Test.

Backup of all systems including data and configuration

It is important to make a full backup of the target system before a scan is carried out. This will ensure if something goes wrong with the target machine due to the vulnerability scan, the latest backup can be restored immediately to put the target machine back. Backup administrators should make sure they perform a full backup, which includes all data, configurations, integration information, code, release notes and special configurations, IOS, and so on.

Updating Nessus plugins

Nessus plugins should be updated with the latest definitions before running the scan; this will make sure your Nessus is loaded with all the latest checks to discover the latest vulnerabilities.

Creating a scan policy as per target system OS and information

A scan policy should be configured before running the scan as per the target system operating systems and environments. The policy should be configured in Nessus accordingly. How to create a policy is illustrated in the next section of this chapter.

Configuring a scan policy to check for an organization's security policy compliance

Every organization has its own security policies. Nessus provides a capability to customize scan policy based on the organization's policy; for example, password complexity. While configuring a Nessus policy, you should be careful to customize the password policy as per the target organization's password policy. An organization's password policy might say any password configured is noncompliant if the password length is less than six characters, whereas other organizations might say less than eight characters is a noncompliance. Nessus gives you the flexibility to customize the policy based on your requirements before you run the scan.

Gathering information of target systems

In the previous chapter, we saw the different phases of Vulnerability Assessment. One of the phases before scanning is gathering information, which is again a prerequisite to the scanning phase. You should gather all the possible information from public websites, Internet, and internal staff (in case of an internal scan or a grey-box scan). This information is useful to tweak your Nessus scan policy to configure or select the required checks based on the information you obtain about the target system, also it will help in mapping the network to include the IP address.

Sufficient network bandwidth to run the scan

It is important to run the scan with a good network bandwidth; if you run the scan on a low bandwidth, there are chances that packets may be dropped in between and your scan may get interrupted in between. To avoid all such circumstances, it is always recommended to run the scan when you have good network bandwidth. This will also help you in timely completion of the scan.

Target system support staff

It is recommended to have target system administrators or an expert support staff to analyze the health and performance of target systems. If they are available during the scanning window, they can continuously monitor target systems and sound alarms. If the system is not performing properly, stop the scan; or if something goes wrong, the system can be recovered.

Policy configuration

Policy configuration is the primary step performed prior to scanning. Policy configuration, in simple terms, means setting up Nessus with the most optimized configuration for scanning based on the target infrastructure.

The key parameters that can be configured while setting up a policy are as follows:

- Name of the policy
- Type of port scanning required
- Performance of scan in terms of maximum checks per scan in parallel and so on, which will decide on the scan time
- Option of entering credentials for the infrastructure being scanned locally

- Option to select the most appropriate plugins
- Advance preference option to provide different drop-down options to choose configuration to further fine tune the policy depending on the target; for example, database-compliance checks, Cisco IOS compliance checks, and so on

Nessus provides an option to upload a scan policy if you already have it from somewhere else. Similarly, the option to export and copy an existing policy is also available. If you have multiple Nessus systems, you may want to use export and upload options to have the same policies on all Nessus systems. You can also delete a policy if you are no longer using it.

Default policy settings

By default, there are four default policy templates that are preloaded in the Nessus scanner; these templates will enable the user to start scanning using these basic policies and to get an idea of how a typical policy configuration will look or to customize them as per our requirement.

The default policies are listed as follows:

- External network scan
- Internal network scan
- PCI DSS audit policy
- Web application testing policy

These policies are self-explanatory. If you want to scan an external network, use the external network scan policy; if you want to scan the internal network, use the internal network scan policy; if you want to conduct a scan for the PCI DSS purpose, use the PCI DSS audit policy, and lastly, if you want to scan an application for web-application-related vulnerabilities, such as cross-site request forgery, cross-site scripting, and SQL injections, use the web application testing policy.

It is recommended to use these default policies as base templates to create your own customized policies. You may want to copy the existing default policy and save it with a new name as per your scanning requirements.

New policy creation

The next section will familiarize you with the different options available while setting up a scan policy in Nessus. To start configuring a new scan policy, click on the **+ New Policy** option under the policy tab. Under this tab, there are four policy setting options available, namely **General Settings**, **Credentials**, **Plugins**, and **Preferences**.

General Settings

The **General Settings** tab enables the user to set general information, such as scan name, scan setting type, and description. The settings available under this setting are basic, port scanning, performance, and advanced.

The **Basic** setting includes the following options:

- **Name**: This option allows assigning a unique name to the policy
- **Visibility**: This option allows the policy to be shared with others or keep for private use; only administrative users are allowed to share the policy
- **Description**: This option provides an option to add a description to the policy for future reference; for example, the description of a policy configured for database scanning can be updated in a way for the user to recall and use the policy as per the purpose it was set for
- **Allow Port- Scan Report Edit**: This option allows you to delete the items in the report post port scanning; typically, this should be disabled while conducting the scan from the compliance perspective to showcase that the report was not tampered, as shown in the following screenshot:

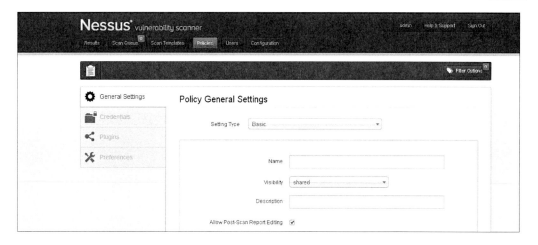

The **Port Scanning** setting includes the following options:

- **Port Scan Range**: It specifies the number of ports to be scanned. **default** indicates 4,790 common ports found in the Nessus-services file, **ALL** indicates all 65,365 ports. A specific port range can also be specified by using the - symbol. Also, scanning different range of ports for TCP and UDP in the same policy can be done using t: and u: followed by a port range. A different range of ports for TCP/UDP in the same policy can be specified using a comma sign; for example, T 90;1000,U:350-400.

- **Consider Unscanned Port as Closed**: If this option is selected in the policy, Nessus will consider the port as closed if Nessus is not able to scan the port.

- **Nessus SNMP Scanner**: It allows Nessus to target the SNMP service while scanning; this is complimented by adding the SNMP setting in the policy's **Preference** section for better scan results.

- **netstat portscanner (SSH)**: This option uses the netstat command available over SSH connection to find open ports in a UNIX system. This command requires authentication credentials.

- **Ping the remote host**: This option helps to find live systems by pinging the ports. Based on the ping response, Nessus will identify it as open.

- **Netstat Port Scanner (WMI)**: This option uses the netstat command available over the WMI connection to find open ports in a Windows system. This command requires authentication credentials.

- **Nessus TCP Scanner**: This option is Nessus in-built option to find open TCP ports.

- **Nessus SYN Scanner**: This option uses Nessus in-built SYN scan feature to identify an open port.

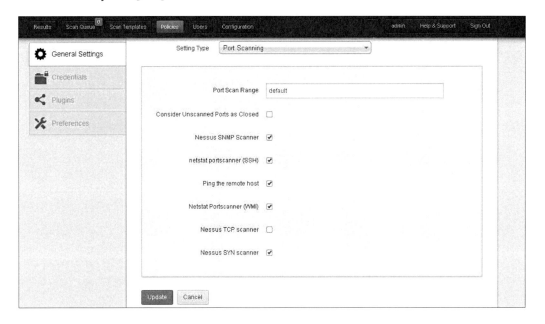

The **Performance** setting includes the following options:

- **Max Checks Per Host**: This option enables Nessus to perform maximum number of checks that Nessus launched against a single target machine at one time.

- **Max Hosts Per Scan**: This option enables Nessus to scan maximum number of hosts Nessus will scan in parallel.

- **Network Receive Timeout (seconds)**: This option shows the maximum time Nessus will wait for a host to respond. This value is set to 5 seconds as default and can also be superseded by the value mentioned in a particular plugin. This can be set to a higher value in case of slow connection.

- **Max Simultaneous TCP Sessions Per Host**: This option limits the maximum number of TCP sessions to a single target machine.

- **Max Simultaneous TCP Sessions Per Scan**: This option limits the maximum number of TCP sessions for the whole period of scanning, no matter how many target machines are scanned.

- **Reduce Parallel Connections on Congestion**: This option enables Nessus to reduce the number of packets being sent on the network to avoid choking the network bandwidth.

- **Use Kernel Congestion Detection (Linux Only)**: This feature is available for Nessus scanners deployed on Linux. Once this option is enabled, Nessus will monitor CPU and other internal parameters and will modify the resource utilization accordingly.

The **Advanced** setting includes the following options:

- **Safe checks**: This option disables plugins, which might have an impact on the target machine. It is important to select this option to run a safe scan.

- **Silent dependencies**: This option, if checked, includes a list of dependencies not in the report.

- **Log Scan Details to Server**: This option logs additional information to the Nessus server log; this helps to evaluate a scan from the plugin's perspective, that is, it helps to determine whether a particular plugin was launched and used.

- **Stop host scan on disconnect**: If this option is enabled, Nessus will stop scanning the target machine, if it feels the target machine is not responding back to the packets being sent. This may happen due to some reason, such as the target machine being turned off or traffic to the target machines is blocked.

- **Avoid sequential scans**: A list of hosts under the scope of scanning can be fed to Nessus; if this option is chosen, Nessus will conduct the scan in a random manner instead of going sequentially.

- **Designate hosts by their DNS name**: This option enables the use of hostname in the report prepared post scanning instead of the IP address of the target machine.

Credentialed scan

Nessus offers a feature to perform credentialed or authenticated scans. With this option, Nessus is able to log in to the local system to find local system level vulnerabilities, such as missing patches and operating system settings. Typically, these vulnerabilities are not highlighted by Nessus in case of a noncredential scan over the network. In short, the credential scan option helps to find local vulnerabilities of the system after logging in to the system using the credential provided. A credential scan performs the same operations as the local user of the system; it depends on the level of access granted to the local user account used by Nessus.

The following screenshot shows the option to configure a credential scan for **Windows credentials, SSH settings, Kerberos configuration**, and **Cleartext protocol settings**:

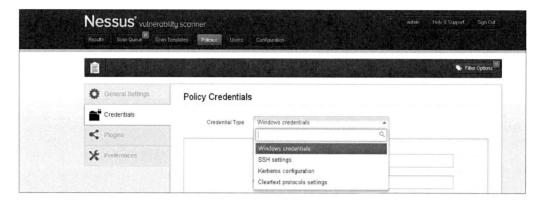

The Windows credentials option

Under the Windows credential option, Nessus captured the **Server Messaging Block** (**SMB**) configuration details. SMB is a file sharing protocol, which will help Nessus to unearth local vulnerabilities in a Windows system. It is always recommended to use an account with administrative privileges for the best possible results of a credentialed scan.

Windows usernames, passwords, and domains

The SMB domain field is optional and Nessus will be able to log in with domain credentials without this field. The username, password, and optional domain refer to an account that the target machine is aware of.

Even if credentials are not used, Nessus will attempt to log in to a Windows server with the following combinations:

- Administrator without a password
- A random username and password to test guest accounts
- No username or password to test null sessions

Nessus supports several different types of authentication methods for Windows-based systems. Each of these methods take a username, password, and domain name (sometimes optional for authentication). The setting option enables you to specify the use of NTLM or Kerberos option.

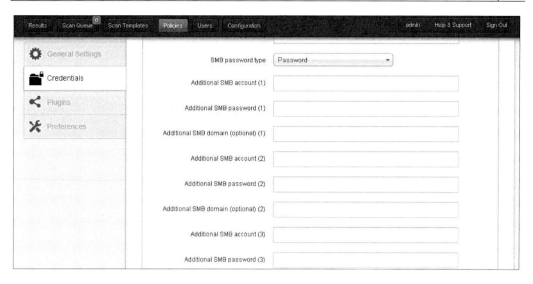

The SSH settings option

The **SSH settings** option from the drop-down menu allows you to enter credentials for scanning UNIX systems. Credentials are used to obtain local information from remote UNIX systems. The field for entering the SSH username for the account will perform the checks on the target UNIX system along with either the SSH password or the SSH public key, and private key pair. There is also a field for entering the passphrase for the SSH key, if it is required.

The most effective credentialed scans are those when the supplied credentials have root privileges. As many sites do not permit a remote login as root, Nessus users can invoke su, sudo, su+sudo, or dzdo with a separate password for an account that has been set up to have su or sudo privileges.

If an SSH known_hosts file is available and provided as part of the scan policy, Nessus will only attempt to log in to hosts in this file. The preferred SSH port can be set to direct Nessus to connect to SSH, if it is running on a port other than 22. If an account, other than root, is to be used for privilege escalation, it can be mentioned under the **Elevate Privileges with** option.

Best practices recommend using SSH keys for authentication rather than SSH passwords. This will assure that the same username and password used for auditing the SSH server are not used to attempt a log in to a system that may not be under your control.

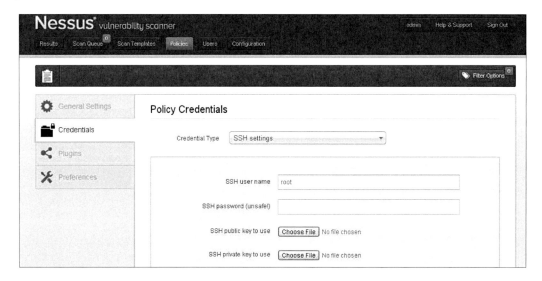

The Kerberos configuration option

The **Kerberos configuration** option allows you to specify credentials using Kerberos keys from a remote system.

The Cleartext protocols settings option

In case a secure encrypted option is not available to do a credential scan, Nessus offers a feature of scan over cleartext protocol for `telnet`, `rsh`, `rexec`. In this option, the password travels unsafely in the Cleartext channel. This option also allows you to check the patching level.

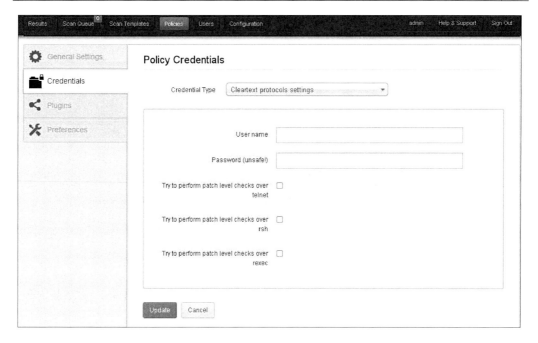

Plugins

Plugins are the files used by Nessus for vulnerability checks. These plugins are updated on a regular basis with the latest vulnerability checks as they become available.

The plugins are divided into product families to enable an accurate and effective grouping of similar plugins together. Thus, by choosing the appropriate plugins family, a large number of applicable/not applicable plugins can be enabled or disabled efficiently and with minimal clicks.

Also, Nessus releases new plugins as and when new vulnerabilities are released.

The following screenshot shows how the **Policy Plugin Configurations** window
will look:

The following table represents the plugin color and their meaning. Basically, this
represents the number of plugins enabled from a particular plugin family.

Color	Meaning
Green	It represents that all the plugins in a family are enabled.
Grey	It represents that all the plugins in the family are disabled.
Blue	It represents a mixed selection where within a plugins family, some of the plugins are selected and some deselected.

The details of plugins selected will also be represented in the report against the
vulnerability found due to a particular plugin.

Filtering

On top of the **Plugins** page, a filtering option is available. This option allows
choosing plugins, which is enabled with a policy by applying filters.

Filters can be added and removed by using the **ADD Filter** and **CLEAR Filters** button, respectively. Nessus also gives a **Match** option with **Any** and **All**. The **Any** option means that any one of the filter options specified is met. The **All** option means that the entire filter condition, which is mentioned should be specified.

By using filter options, the most optimized scanning plugins can be chosen. Also, it is recommended to first display all filters and apply the policy using the filtering option.

The details of the different plugin families and filtration criteria can be looked into in the *Tenable documentation*:

> *"The "Denial of Service" family contains some plugins that could cause outages on a network if the "Safe Checks" option is not enabled, but does contain some useful checks that will not cause any harm. The "Denial of Service" family can be used in conjunction with "Safe Checks" to ensure that any potentially dangerous plugins are not run. However, it is recommended that the "Denial of Service" family not be used on a production network."*

Preferences

Preferences are the deeper settings of a Nessus policy, which are dynamic in nature. Dynamic means the options in the drop-down menu to configure preference settings may vary depending on the plugins and feed license.

These settings can be chosen by the person creating the scan policy depending on the target system's requirement. For example, if you plan to scan a database then while creating the policy, select **Database Settings** from the **Preferences** drop-down menu. This particular setting allows you to key in database details with the database credentials to probe the database further. This will allow your Nessus scan to discover more vulnerability.

I recommend the Nessus website, `http://www.tenable.com`, for the latest settings and their explanations.

Scan configuration

A sequential reading of this chapter is required for readers before jumping into this section. In the previous sections, we have explained the prerequisites one should take care of before running a scan. Also, it has been discussed how a scan policy should be configured and customized as per the target organizations security policy and what the differences are between a credential and a noncredential scan.

Configuring a new scan

How to initiate and execute a scan is illustrated in this section. To initiate a scan, we assume that the scan prerequisites that were previously mentioned in this chapter have been executed. For initiating a scan, log in to Nessus by using your Nessus credentials and click on **Scan Queue** from the uppermost bar of Nessus.

The **Scan Queue** bar has two buttons, namely **New Scan** and **Options**, which is a drop-down menu that provides you with options to resume a scan, pause a scan, or stop a running scan. Click on the **New Scan** button to initiate a new scan.

This has two options in the left-most panel, one for general settings and an other for e-mail settings.

General settings

General settings are the settings of a new scan such as what will be the name of the scan, do you want to run it now or save it as a template, which scan can be run later or you may want to schedule a scan for a desired time, and on which scan it will automatically take place. You can also select the policy which you want to use for this new scan from the policy's drop-down menu. Also, this is the place where you provide IPs that you want to scan. This also provides you with the ability to upload a file, which has a list of IPs to be scanned during this new scan.

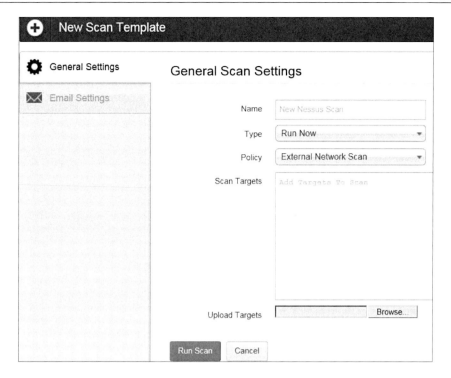

The following table describes the settings given in the preceding screenshot:

General scan setting	Description
Name	How you want to name your scan
Type	This has the following three options in a drop-down menu: • **Run Now**: If you want to run the scan right now • **Template**: If you want to save the scan as a template that you can run later • **Scheduled**: If you want to schedule the scan for a desired time, the scan will initiate automatically at this time
Policy	This is again a drop-down menu that lists all your Nessus scan policies. We discussed about creating a policy in the previous section. This policy should be selected from the drop-down menu, which will be used for the scan.
Scan Targets	All IPs, which need to be scanned should be listed here.
Upload Targets	If you have a text file, which has a list of IPs to be scanned, the same can be imported here in Nessus.

In the end, you have a **Run Scan** button that will initiate the scan.

E-mail settings

E-mail settings can be configured for a scan if your Nessus is configured with an SMTP server. This is used to e-mail the scan results automatically post completion. Recipients' e-mail IDs can be keyed in here in the **Recipient(s)** input box. Also, report filters can be configured. In this case, results will be e-mailed to the recipients if the report filter matches, as shown in the following screenshot:

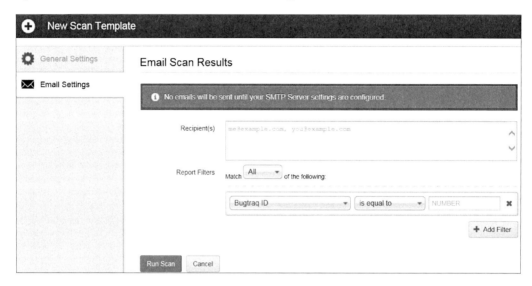

The following table describes the settings given in the previous screenshot:

Email Scan Result Settings	Description
Recipient(s)	To whom you want to send the automated e-mails of the scan results, e-mail IDs of the recipients to be given here.
Report Filters	Report filters can be configured here to match a particular condition or filter. If that matches, an automated e-mail of the result will trigger to the recipients.

At the end, you have a **Run Scan** button that will initiate the scan.

Scan execution and results

In the previous section, we have seen how a scan should be initiated. Once you click on **Run Scan**, the scan takes place.

Results of completed scans can be seen under the **Results** tab. A double-click on the scan result will open the detailed view of a particular scan result. This has three different tabs, namely **Hosts**, **Vulnerabilities**, and **Export results**. Under the **Hosts** tab, the host summary can be seen. This has a severity-wise count (critical, high, medium, low, and informational) of vulnerabilities.

The following screenshot shows that a host is scanned, which has 37 critical, 130 high, 140 medium, 0 low, and 49 informational vulnerabilities:

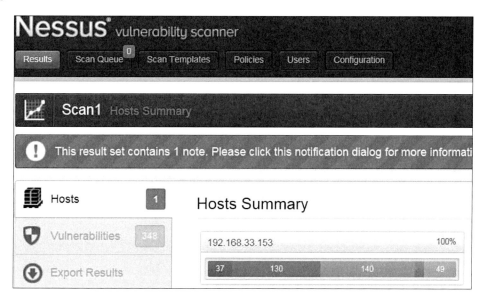

The next tab is **Vulnerabilities**; this shows the vulnerabilities' summary with the risk severity of each vulnerability. Double-clicking on any vulnerability will take you to a detailed view of that vulnerability, which details synopsis, description, solution, vulnerability web links, plugin information, risk information, vulnerability information, reference information, plugin output, and so on. A risk severity modification option is also available in the detailed view.

The final tab is **Export Results**; this provides an option to export a Nessus scan results report in different formats, such as HTML, PDF, and CSV. One can also select what is required to be included in the report from the following options:

- Host summary and executive summary
- Vulnerabilities by host
- Vulnerabilities by plugin
- Compliance check executive
- Compliance check

One or many of these options can be chosen depending on the requirements.

A few sections of this chapter have been referenced from the learning material available on Nessus website: `http://www.tenable.com`.

Summary

In this chapter, we learned to set up Nessus for vulnerability scanning. Scan configuration in Nessus involves two major steps, namely configuration of a scan policy and launching a scan using the configured policy.

Scan prerequisites including deciding on the scope of the scan, getting approval in place, deciding on the scan window, updating plugins, making a backup, having proper network access opened, identifying the point of contact, and deciding on credential or noncredential scanning were also discussed.

Among the prerequisites, the first key step is to set up the scan policy, which will include four default policy templates (external, internal, PCI DSS, and web application). Nessus also offers an option to create a customized policy using the **New Policy** option.

There are four setting options available while creating a new policy, namely **General Settings** and **Advance settings** (including the name of the policy, visibility, port scanning options, scan performance, and safe checks), credentialed scan (with this option, Nessus is able to log in to the local system to find local system level vulnerabilities, such as missing patches, and operating system settings). The options available to add credentials for different infrastructures is explained under this section, **Plugins** (includes choosing the right family of security check based on the type of infrastructure under scope of scanning, such as Windows, Cisco, and database). The Denial of Service plugin should be avoided, unless specifically asked for, as it may cause downtime. The **Preferences** menu includes advance and deeper level of settings, which should be configured as per the infrastructure under scan.

Setting up of a policy is followed by actual scanning; the key activities include choosing a new scan, the **General settings** options that include **Name**, **Type**, and **Policy** for scanning, which can be default or customized, and **Scan targets** including the IP of the infrastructure to be scanned (a text file can be used for the same). It is also explained how scan result can be mailed post completion of a scan. Finally, an option to retrieve the scan result from the **Result** tab is explained in brief.

In the next chapter, we will learn about performing scan results analysis, which will cover false positive analysis, vulnerability analysis, exploiting vulnerabilities, and so on.

3
Scan Analysis

Vulnerability scan analysis is the next step to scanning. For a vulnerability scan assessment to be successful and effective, an accurate analysis of vulnerabilities is absolutely necessary. As most of the scanners produce the scan output in line with the vulnerability plugins available in its repository, a human analysis is highly recommended to avoid false positives and false negatives. In general, a false positive or a false negative represent a scenario where vulnerabilities are either inaccurately reported or not reported at all in the scan output. The definitions are as follows:

- **False positive**: More commonly encountered, this term means vulnerabilities reported as active in the system do not exist in reality; this means it may be a result of incorrect vulnerability reporting
- **False negative**: An output in a vulnerability scan will essentially mean that a vulnerability that exists in reality in the infrastructure is not reported in the scan output

In this chapter, we will learn how to effectively analyze the output of the Nessus scan result by covering the following topics:

- Result analysis
- False positive analysis
- Vulnerability analysis
- Vulnerability exploitation

Result analysis

In the previous chapter of this book, we learnt about performing and saving the scan result. This section covers how to read and interpret the Nessus scan report. For the purpose of illustration, a sample report is used for highlighting the vulnerabilities in a Linux system. The report we use for reference is saved in the HTML format and includes details such as **Hosts Summary**, **Vulnerabilities By Host**, and **Vulnerabilities By Plugin**, which were chosen while saving the report.

Report interpretation

Nessus offers different options such as HTML, PDF, and **comma-separated values** (**CSV**) to save a report. While saving the report—to get the summary and details by vulnerability or host—both the options should be selected.

A typical **Nessus Scan Report** in HTML format is shown in the following screenshot:

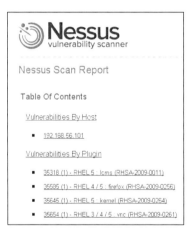

Hosts Summary (Executive)

The **Hosts Summary (Executive)** section will include the count of vulnerabilities against each critical category along with a summarized details of each vulnerability; this includes the following:

- **Severity** (severity rating along with the CVSS score): This defines how critical the observed vulnerability is

- **Plugin Id**: This is the unique identifier for the plugin to check against which vulnerability it was found

- **Name**: This displays the name of the vulnerability

The following screenshot displays a sample report showing the host's summary:

Vulnerabilities By Host

The **Vulnerabilities By Host** section of the report gives a summary of the vulnerability findings per host. The **Summary** gives details about the scan running time, basic details about the host scanned, and the count of the number of vulnerabilities grouped together by the critical rating.

The following screenshot is a sample report showing the host's summary:

The preceding screenshot displays the **Vulnerabilities By Host** option with the following sections:

- **Scan Information**: This section displays the scan's **Start time** and **End time** in the day/time/year format.

- **Host Information**: This section displays the **DNS Name, IP, MAC Address,** and **OS**.

- **Results Summary**: This section gives a count of the vulnerabilities that are grouped together as per the criticality rating assigned by Nessus. These categories are **Critical, High, Medium, Low,** and **Info**. It also shows the **Total** count of vulnerabilities reported by Nessus.

Common Vulnerability Scoring System (CVSS)

Based on the scoring system, Nessus uses **Common Vulnerability Scoring System (CVSS)** to rate vulnerabilities. This is an open source vulnerability-rating system based on the characteristics and impact of vulnerability. It includes parameters such as the intrinsic features of vulnerability, features of vulnerability that change over time, and the characteristics of vulnerability that are specific to an environment. Details of the same can be found at http://www.first.org/cvss/cvss-guide.

The following table lists the CVSS scores based on the vulnerability rating used by Nessus. As explained earlier in this chapter, the rating reported by Nessus can be analyzed further as follows:

CVSS score	Criticality
0	Info
<4	Low
<7	Medium
<10	High
10	Critical

CVSS scores are referenced from different content available over Internet, including Nessus user guide available at `http://www.tenable.com`.

Vulnerabilities By Plugin

The **Vulnerabilities By Plugin** section contains all the relevant details about the vulnerability. The following section displays a screenshot with the details captured for describing the vulnerability, along with a brief explanation of each field.

The following screenshot is for illustration purposes only; additional reference links and **Common Vulnerability and Exposures** (CVE) have been removed:

35585 (1) - RHEL 4 / 5 : firefox (RHSA-2009-0256)

Synopsis

The remote Red Hat host is missing one or more security updates.

Description

An updated firefox package that fixes various security issues is now available for Red Hat Enterprise Linux 4 and 5.

This update has been rated as having critical security impact by the Red Hat Security Response Team.

Mozilla Firefox is an open source Web browser.

Several flaws were found in the processing of malformed web content. A web page containing malicious content could cause Firefox to crash or, potentially, execute arbitrary code as the user running Firefox.
(CVE-2009-0352, CVE-2009-0353, CVE-2009-0356)

Several flaws were found in the way malformed content was processed. A website containing specially-crafted content could, potentially, trick a Firefox user into surrendering sensitive information.
(CVE-2009-0354, CVE-2009-0355)

A flaw was found in the way Firefox treated HTTPOnly cookies. An attacker able to execute arbitrary JavaScript on a target site using HTTPOnly cookies may be able to use this flaw to steal the cookie.
(CVE-2009-0357)

A flaw was found in the way Firefox treated certain HTTP page caching directives. A local attacker could steal the contents of sensitive pages which the page author did not intend to be cached.
(CVE-2009-0358)

For technical details regarding these flaws, please see the Mozilla security advisories for Firefox 3.0.6. You can find a link to the Mozilla advisories in the References section.

All Firefox users should upgrade to these updated packages, which contain Firefox version 3.0.6, which corrects these issues. After installing the update, Firefox must be restarted for the changes to take effect.

The following screenshot displays **References** and the **CVSS Base Score** in the report:

See Also	
https://www.redhat.com/security/data/cve/CVE-2009-0352.html	
https://www.redhat.com/security/data/cve/CVE-2009-0353.html	
https://www.redhat.com/security/data/cve/CVE-2009-0354.html	
https://www.redhat.com/security/data/cve/CVE-2009-0355.html	
XREF	OSVDB:51940
XREF	RHSA:2009-0256
XREF	CWE:200
CVSS Base Score	
10.0 (CVSS2#AV:N/AC:L/Au:N/C:C/I:C/A:C)	
References	
CVE	CVE-2009-0352
CVE	CVE-2009-0353
CVE	CVE-2009-0354
XREF	OSVDB:51940
XREF	RHSA:2009-0256
XREF	CWE:200

The following screenshot displays the **Plugin Information** section:

```
Plugin Information:
Publication date: 2009/02/04, Modification date: 2013/05/11
Hosts
192.168.56.101 (tcp/0)

Remote package installed : firefox-3.0.5-1.el5_2
Should be : firefox-3.0.6-1.el5

Remote package installed : nss-3.12.2.0-2.el5
Should be : nss-3.12.2.0-4.el5
```

The vulnerability details which are captured in the preceding screenshots are as follows:

Vulnerability parameter	Details
Synopsis	This section displays the key characteristics of the vulnerability. For example, here, the synopsis section describes the missing security patch.
Description	This section gives details about the vulnerability and includes key security issues that exist because of the identified vulnerability. For example, a key security issue because of a missing patch along with the CVE number is mentioned in the screenshot. High-level recommendation is also covered in this section.

Vulnerability parameter	Details
See Also	This section contains reference links (if any) useful for better understanding of the issue released by the vendor of the component/infrastructure where the vulnerability is found.
Solution	This section gives recommendations for vulnerability mitigation.
Risk Factor	This section displays the risk rating of the identified vulnerabilities. For example, **Critical**, **High**, and **Medium**.
CVSS Base Score	This section displays the CVSS score based on which the risk rating is calculated.
References	This section displays the CVE and CWE information of the issues observed. XREF is a cross-reference to other information sources related to the vulnerability.
Plugin Information	This section displays details about the plugin that enables the finding of this vulnerability.
Host	This section displays the IP address of the host on which this vulnerability is observed along with the current and suggested details regarding the infrastructure on which the vulnerability was observed.

Common Vulnerability and Exposures (**CVE**) is a database of publicly known security vulnerabilities and exposures. Each vulnerability is assigned a unique CVE number, which is cross-referenced in the Nessus report for providing further details about the vulnerability. For further information, refer to http://cve.mitre.org.

Common Weakness Enumeration (**CWE**) is a dictionary of common weakness types, which gives details about various commonly known vulnerabilities. This is also referenced by Nessus for better understanding of the vulnerabilities. For further information, refer to http://cwe.mite.org.

False positive analysis

False positive refers to the issues or vulnerabilities highlighted by any scanning tool, but which don't actually exist on the target system. The false positive rate differs from tool to tool; the few common pointers that can be considered for a false positive analysis are listed as follows.

Understanding an organization's environment

The following are the basic understandings of an organization that will aid in the false positive analysis:

- Basic organization infrastructure details, such as the network landscape, infrastructure, OS, application, and technology used, will help cross-check the Vulnerability Assessment (VA) result against the technology and versions actually implemented to remove a false positive

- This becomes more beneficial in situations where the VA scan in a periodic cycle uses the internal infrastructure where these details are readily available

- In case of a time-bound scanning done as an external consultant, it is difficult to have access to all such details. In such cases, as a part of the pre-engagement prerequisites, access to relevant infrastructure stakeholders can be sought for understanding the technology details

Target-critical vulnerabilities

In case of a large number of vulnerabilities, at least the most critical ones should be cross-verified for a false positive before being reported.

Proof of concept

If there is access to servers/devices on which the VA scan is conducted, vulnerabilities can be crosschecked by logging in to the server or by trying to put a proof of concept against the vulnerability. For example, if the vulnerability states that a clear text **File Transfer Protocol (FTP)** or Telnet service is running in the server, we can either log in to the server to crosscheck if these services are actually running, or give a proof of concept by trying to connect FTP or the Telnet protocol from the testing machine.

Port scanning tools

Open source scanning tools such as **Nmap** can also be used to enumerate the infrastructure again for open vulnerabilities to cross-check the findings of the VA report.

Effort estimation

As effort estimation is a time consuming activity, additional efforts and resources should be considered to include the removal of a false positive. Also, based on the size and nature of engagement, a practical call should be taken to define the extent to which this activity will be done.

Vulnerability analysis

In general terminologies, vulnerability analysis is considered similar to vulnerability assessment. However, I feel there is a small difference between these two. Vulnerability analysis is a part of the vulnerability assessment cycle, where you identify the vulnerability, quantify the risk, and prioritize the risk. Vulnerability analysis investigates the vulnerabilities that are detected by a vulnerability assessment tool.

It should be noted that vulnerability analysis is an optional step that depends on the vulnerability assessment tool's capability, scanning environment, in-depth analysis, and so on. Investigation of vulnerability should be done considering all these factors. Nowadays, most of the vulnerability assessment tools fetch automated reports that have no or minimal false positives. Nessus is one of these.

When a vulnerability assessment is done by a **security operation center** (**SOC**) or an internal security department where you don't want to put much effort in doing manual analysis, you prefer to give all the scan results to the different teams for vulnerability closure. In this case, you are not very concerned about the severity of the vulnerability, and so on. If we talk about a different scenario where you are engaged with a firm as a third-party auditor and you are doing a vulnerability assessment, then in this case, each vulnerability you report to the firm will be taken very seriously and has to have proper justifications for the vulnerability's existence, severity, applicability, and so on.

In this section, we will explore the second scenario mentioned previously that talks about a third-party consultant doing an audit or a technical vulnerability assessment for a client, where a vulnerability report needs to be perfect in terms of applicability, risk severity, environment dependencies, and no false positives.

Once you get the scan result report from a vulnerability scanner such as Nessus, you can do a detailed review of each vulnerability to check at least the following areas:

- False positives
- Risk severity
- Applicability analysis
- Fix recommendations

False positives

The second section of this chapter details false positive analysis.

Risk severity

Risk severity is the severity of the risk associated with each vulnerability, depending on the environment and nature of the business. Risk severity can be quantitative or qualitative. Generally, it is preferred, and industry-wise recognized, to use risk severity as qualitative. Risk can be categorized as **Critical**, **High**, **Medium**, **Low**, and **Info**. A few organizations categorize them only as **High**, **Moderate**, and **Low**.

Most of the large-enterprise organizations that go through different security certifications, such as ISO 27001, have their risk management process defined. These risk management processes define their risk severities as well as their definitions, risk matrix, risk acceptance criteria, and so on. While performing a vulnerability assessment, you may need to recategorize the risk severity ratings if you follow the risk matrix.

For example, vulnerability on the public website of an organization that is running without SSL. This vulnerability might be declared to have a **High** risk rating by a vulnerability scanner, where-as, if you do a vulnerability analysis, it may declare a different risk level.

Let's take a scenario where you are doing a vulnerability assessment for a small NGO; they have no sensitive information on their website and the vulnerability of SSL is discovered. All information available on the website is public. In this scenario, you may say the vulnerability risk rating is **Low** or **Info**, whereas the scanning tool might report it as **High**.

In a different scenario, where you are doing vulnerability assessment for a medium-sized firm which does surveys on their website and public reports, the same vulnerability of SSL is discovered. Most of the information recorded here is confidential and should not be compromised. In this scenario, you can say that the vulnerability risk rating is **Medium** or **High** and will be rated as **High** by the scanning tool.

Another scenario where you are doing a vulnerability assessment for a large bank, which has net banking login on their website. Bank customers log in to use the net banking service and do their financial transactions; again, the same SSL vulnerability is discovered. In this case, if SSL is not implemented, this is a critical risk rating vulnerability, and the tool will report it as **High**.

It is very important for us to relook at the risk ratings given by vulnerability scanning tools if we want to treat risks based on their risk ratings.

Applicability analysis

Each vulnerability discovered by vulnerability assessment tools may not be applicable to the organization. Vulnerability applicability is used for checking if the vulnerability reported by an automated vulnerability-assessment tool is applicable to the organization or not.

For example, vulnerability such as a weak password existing in an application. This vulnerability might be declared to have a **High** risk rating by a vulnerability scanner, where-as, if you do vulnerability applicability analysis, it may be declared as not applicable.

Let's take a scenario where you are doing the vulnerability assessment of a small organization. The vulnerability scanner reports weak password vulnerability for an application. It is found by the tool that some of the passwords for that application were only seven-characters long, which is reported as a **High** risk severity vulnerability. While doing an applicability analysis, we found that the organization has approved a security password policy that considers a password as strong even if it is seven-characters long; hence, this vulnerability is not applicable to the organization.

It is important to relook at the risks and see if they are really applicable for the organization or not.

Fix recommendations

Nessus gives fix recommendations in the tool-generated report for each vulnerability. A few of them can be fixed using multiple ways, for instance, by using compensatory controls. A vulnerability can be patched or fixed in multiple ways.

Let us illustrate this through a sample vulnerability. A vulnerability such as the cleartext protocol FTP is found open on a server. The fix usually recommended is used as a secured protocol for file transfer such as **Secure File Transfer Protocol (SFTP)**. Another solution may be to analyze the requirement of having FTP open. There might be a case where FTP was left open during testing; now even in production, FTP is open and is no longer in use. In this case, the FTP port should be closed on that server. In this scenario, we see that for the same vulnerability there are two fixes: one is to use SFTP instead of FTP, another is to close the FTP port. Likewise, it is recommended to apply the fixes wisely.

Vulnerability exploiting

In *Chapter 1*, *Fundamentals*, we covered the differences between a vulnerability assessment and a penetration testing exercise. Basically, the difference between these two is related to exploiting the vulnerabilities. In a vulnerability assessment, you are required to discover the vulnerabilities only; but in a penetration test, you are also required to exploit the vulnerabilities that you found during the vulnerability scan.

Penetration testing may not necessarily be intrusive; it can also be limited to the proof of concepts. Nowadays, most of the organizations want to have their pentest (penetration test) scope limited only till the proof of concepts are produced, because if you do an intrusive test, your system/service may go down.

There are multiple penetration testing tools available in the market that are equipped with scripts, programs, payloads, and injections, for carrying out penetration testing.

The following are a few examples showing how a vulnerability can be exploited. The following vulnerabilities have been reported by a Nessus scanner on a sample machine.

Exploit example 1

A vulnerability title is of the first example is a **Cross-site scripting (XSS)** found on an application homepage.

Let's take a scenario where the vulnerability scan resulted in a vulnerability of XSS for one of the applications scanned while running on a target host. Details for the XSS are given in the following Nessus report, reflecting on which application the page vulnerability exists:

Nessus report head	Nessus report example text
Synopsis	The remote web server hosts a PHP script that is prone to a cross-site scripting attack.
Description	The version of phpMyAdmin fails to validate BBcode tags in user input to the `error` parameter of the `error.php` script before using it to generate dynamic HTML.
	An attacker may be able to leverage this issue by injecting arbitrary HTML or script code into a user's browser to be executed within the security context of the affected site. For example, this could be used to display a page with arbitrary text and a link to an external site.
Solution	Upgrade to phpMyAdmin 3.4.0-beta1 or later.
See Also	`http://www.phpmyadmin.net/home_page/security/PMASA-2010-9.php`

Nessus report head	Nessus report example text
Plugin Information	Publication date: January 6, 2011, Modification date: October 24, 2011
Risk Information	Medium
	4.3 (CVSS2#AV:N/AC:M/Au:N/C:N/I:P/A:N)
	3.6 (CVSS2#AV:N/AC:M/Au:N/C:N/I:P/A:N)
Vulnerability Information	Cross-site scripting allows an attacker to run scripts that may lead to stealing the web browser session information or creating web links to deface the web application.
References Information	BID 45633
	CVE CVE-2010-4480
	XREF OSVDB:69684
	XREF EDB-ID:15699
Plugin Output	Nessus is able to exploit the issue using the following URL:
	`http://192.168.56.3/phpMyAdmin/error.php?type=phpmyadmin_pmasa_2010_9.nasl&error=%5ba%40http%3a%2f%2fwww.phpmyadmin.net%2fhome_page%2fsecurity%2fPMASA-2010-9.php%40_self]Click%20here%5b%2fa]`

Once a cross-site scripting is reported by a vulnerability scanner, and if you are engaged to conduct penetration testing for that machine, you are required to further penetrate the vulnerability. This can be done by running malicious scripts, to do the proof of concept, and by exploitation.

Cross-site scripting, which is also known as XSS, can either be in an input parameter that takes some input in the URL or be in one of the input boxes on the web application. To exploit it, you need to tamper the end user's input that goes in the parameter which further displays the same input. You may want to use a tools such as Burp Suits, Bayden Tamper IE, or any other HTTP traffic interceptor. By using the interceptor, you can fiddle with the HTTP request going from the client machine to the server.

To test if XSS exists or not, the following sample payloads can be used as input to the end user's input parameters:

```
<script>alert("XSS Exist")</Script>
"><script>alert("XSS Exist")</Script>
```

The preceding payloads need to be tweaked based on the code which you are exploiting.

To penetrate further, you can use the following sample payloads:

```
<script>alert(document.cookie)</script>
onmouseenter="alert(document.cookie);
onreadystatechange="alert(document.cookie);
```

This will pop up the live cookie details on the screen, as shown in the following screenshot:

In case of persistent XSS, where end user inputs get stored in the database and are displayed again for all users from the database while browsing the application page. You should try the following payload, which creates a hyperlink on the web page, which will redirect the user to the attacker's website:

```
http://TargetIP:8080/ShowingImage.asp?id=<img%20src=
   "http://attackerURL.com/images/1/419979.JPG">
<a href = "http://www.attackerURL.com">click</a>
```

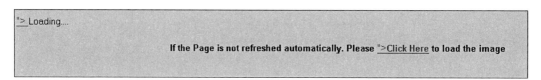

XSS can be exploited further with a deep understanding of scripts and coding.

Exploit example 2

The vulnerability title for the second example is exploitation of weak or easily guessable passwords found on the router.

Nessus has the capability to review Cisco device configurations against industry's best practices. One of the common vulnerabilities, which can be observed when the administrator has not carefully configured the Cisco device, is using default or weak passwords.

Cisco Internetwork Operating System (**Cisco IOS**) is the operating system for Cisco network devices such as routers and switches. We will take the example of a router for illustration purposes. The Cisco router configuration files have all the relevant configurations for the router to perform it's routing functionality in the network.

Cisco IOS provides an option to set different types of password: type 0 typically means a password with no encryption, type 7 means a password encrypted using service password encryption command, which uses a proprietary algorithm, and type 5 means the password is protected with the enabled-secret command, which uses MD5 hashing in the configuration. When we see type 5 or type 7 passwords in the Cisco router configuration, they will appear as encrypted.

```
service password-encryption
hostname Router
enable secret 5 $1$2ZTf$9UBtjkoYo6vW'
username admin privilege 15 password 7 0822455D0A16
```

A Cisco type 7 password is not considered to be safe, as it is encrypted using a weak algorithm, and can be cracked.

While scanning the Cisco router configuration by providing credentials with appropriate privileges, Nessus will highlight the use of a weak password.

It can be exploited once the Nessus report highlights the use of a weak type 7 password and can be cracked further using one of the many freeware utilities available on the Internet. For demonstration purpose, following URL is used:

`http://www.ibeast.com/content/tools/CiscoPassword/index.asp`

If the Nessus highlight uses of weak or type 7 passwords post scanning of the Cisco router; we have used a type 7 password used in our example (`0822455D0A16`).

If we take this password and use the preceding link to crack it, within a few seconds we will come to know that the default password, that is, **cisco**, has been used.

In the following screenshot, we enter a type 7 password in a commonly available password cracking tool:

The following screenshot displays the tool giving the output (cracked password):

Exploit example 3

The vulnerability title for the third example is possible SQL Injection.

SQL Injection is an application vulnerability which can be discovered by Nessus. SQL Injection allows an attacker to inject or run a malicious SQL command by which the attacker directly communicates with the database running behind the application and executes the SQL queries. This can be as destructive as running an `fdisk` command on a database server which will completely format the server, and creating a local admin on the server will compromise the server in all aspects. This also allows an attacker to run extended stored procedures, which are very powerful commands. By running malicious SQL queries, the attacker can modify the input strings that form the SQL queries in such a way that the outputs will reveal the required schema and data from the database.

When a SQL Injection vulnerability is reported by the vulnerability scanner and you are engaged in doing a penetration test, you need to exploit it further.

The following is the process for exploitation:

On the application login page, where the username and password need to be entered, use the input injections, mentioned in the following table, to check if a SQL Injection really exists for that particular page:

Serial number	Injection strings
1	Username: `admin` (any username)
	Password: `' OR 1=1--`
2	Username: `admin'; --`
	Password: `' OR 1=1--`
3	Username: `administrator'; --`
	Password: `' OR 1=1--`

All exploits are unique in nature, hence, I recommend to construct your injections, scripts, and payloads depending on your target machine.

Summary

Scan analysis includes analysis of the scan output to ensure validated and accurate reporting of vulnerabilities. This includes removing false positives and false negatives.

A false positive is more commonly encountered; this term means vulnerabilities reported as active in the system do not exist in reality, which means it may be the result of incorrect vulnerability reporting.

A false positive can be removed by understanding an organization's environment, proof of concept, and validating using port scanning tools. As it is a time consuming activity, it can be done using target-critical vulnerabilities for a big scope engagement. Effort estimation for this activity should also be considered in advance.

Result analysis includes going through the Nessus scan output, covering all necessary details, such as synopsis, description, risk factor including the CVE score, which is a database of publicly-known security vulnerabilities and exposure. Each vulnerability is assigned a unique CVE number which is cross-referenced in the Nessus report for providing further details about the vulnerability.

Apart from removing the false positive, analysis will also involve severity analysis based on the criticality of the system with respect to the organization's business needs where a low or medium vulnerability, on a highly critical server, needs to be prioritized accordingly. The applicability of a particular reported vulnerability to an organization should also be cross-checked.

Based on the recommendation given in the report and considering other alternative controls available to mitigate the vulnerability, the closures should be worked upon.

Vulnerability exploitation (or penetration testing) is the next step after the identification of a vulnerability. Nessus gives an option to check if the exploit of an identified vulnerability is available in exploit frameworks such as **Metasploit** or **Canvas**. It also involves further learning and research to choose an appropriate payload in the case of few vulnerabilities such as cross-site scripting and SQL Injection.

4
Reporting Options

Easy-to-understand and impressive reporting is the key to a successful Vulnerability Assessment. It is very important to understand who the target audience is before you write a Vulnerability Assessment report. Most of the time, a Vulnerability Assessment report will be read by different groups and by audiences at varying levels of proficiency. Some of them may have very strong knowledge about technical terms and some may not understand anything technical; hence, it's important that the report have the right mix of material that addresses both technical and non-technical audiences. It is important to generate a comprehensive Vulnerability Assessment report to make others aware of the vulnerabilities found in the text format so that it is easy to understand for the target readers.

This chapter will show you how to write a successful vulnerability report. The key areas that will be covered in this chapter are as follows:

- Report generation
- Report customization
- Report automation

Vulnerability Assessment report

What to include and what not to include in a vulnerability assessment or penetration testing report has always been a subject of discussion. It is important for you to understand that a Vulnerability Assessment will not achieve its objective without a good report.

The report should be written keeping the audience in mind. In most of the cases, Vulnerability Assessment reports are distributed to different teams in a big enterprise, with different levels of understanding about the report.

A management professional is not interested in looking into the details of each vulnerability. They would rather see a summary of the assessment with a quick screenshot of the number of vulnerabilities that have been identified, categorized by their severity; this can be better captured in a graphical representation along with some text around the section showing critical/high/medium/low severity vulnerabilities. On the other hand, a technical person would like to see more technical details about the vulnerability report and a step-by-step procedure, in case it is a penetration testing report; this will help them reproduce the vulnerability. A technical person would also like to receive recommendations on how to fix the vulnerability.

Nessus generates a report of the successful scan, which captures details about each vulnerability. Depending on the audience, the report can be customized. It is recommended to choose and apply appropriate filters to decide on report content if you perform the scan very often and want to produce the report in the same format each time. Security consultants may not want to do that since they get different reporting requirements from different clients.

Nessus report generation

Nessus generates reports for all completed scans, which can be exported to the local system and it allows you to generate reports from previous scans as well. Multiple formats of the report are available in Nessus, that can be chosen while generating the report.

After completing a scan, Nessus stores the scan results. Nessus stores scan results under the **Results** tab as shown in the following screenshot:

A double-click on the scan result will show the detailed view of that particular scan result. This view has three different tabs: **Hosts**, **Vulnerabilities**, and **Export Results**. Under the **Hosts** tab, the host summary can be seen. This has the severity-wise (critical, high, medium, low, and informational) count of the vulnerabilities.

The following screenshot shows that a host has been scanned, which has thirty-seven critical, one hundred and thirty high, one hundred and forty medium, zero low, and forty-nine informational vulnerabilities:

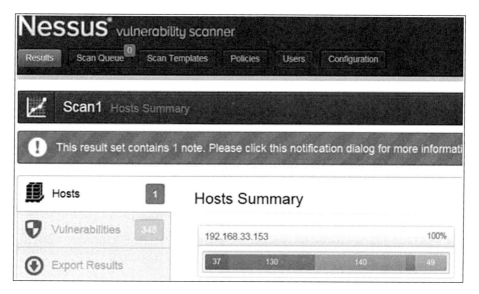

The next tab is the **Vulnerabilities** tab; this shows the vulnerabilities summary with the risk severity of each vulnerability. Double-clicking on any vulnerability will take you to a detailed view of that vulnerability, which details the synopsis, description, solution, vulnerability web links, plugin information, risk information, vulnerability information, reference information, plugin output, and so on. A risk severity modification option is also available in the detailed view. The following screenshot shows a vulnerability summary view:

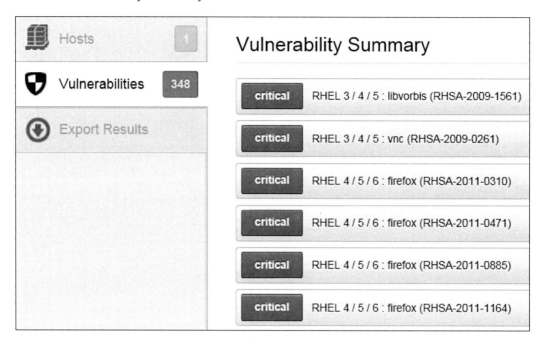

The last tab is **Export Results**; this provides an option to export a Nessus scan result report in different formats, such as HTML, PDF, and CSV. You can also select what requires to be included in the report from the following options:

- **Hosts Summary (Executive)**: This option will export a report that shows a high-level summary of the vulnerabilities discovered
- **Vulnerabilities By Host**: This option will export a report that shows the vulnerabilities by host
- **Compliance Checks (Executive)**: This option will export a report that shows an executive summary related to the selected compliance checks
- **Vulnerabilities By Plugin**: This option will export a report that shows the vulnerabilities by plugin
- **Compliance Checks**: This option will export a report that shows details related to the selected compliance checks

The preceding options can be seen in the following screenshot:

One or more options can be chosen, depending on the need.

Nessus provides you with an option to remove or delete a vulnerability before you export the reports so that if you know that vulnerability is not applicable to you, you can remove or delete it from the Nessus vulnerability list.

Report filtering option

At the top of the **Results** page, a filtering option is available. This option allows you to filter a Nessus report based on the few available criteria you select from the drop-down menu. You can add multiple filters at a time.

For example, you can add multiple filters by choosing the options in the filter drop-down menu to get the report with vulnerabilities, which have a high risk factor, can be exploitable with Exploit Available in MetaSploit and exploitability ease is Exploit Available.

The following screenshot shows how to add a filter:

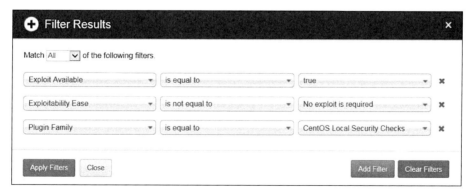

Filters can be added and removed using the **Add Filter** and **Clear Filters** buttons, respectively. Nessus also gives a **Match** option with **Any** and **All** conditions. The **Any** condition indicates whether or not any one of the filter options specified is met. The **All** condition indicates that all the filter conditions set should be met.

Other options in the Nessus reporting tool are for comparing the results of two scans and audit trails. Nessus also allows you to upload the scan results from a different machine, using which you can generate reports as per your need.

Nessus report content

The Nessus report contains a lot of details about the scan and vulnerabilities. Information about the scan is in the form of a list of scanned IPs, the scan's start time and end time, DNS name, Mac address, operating system, and a result summary that gives an overall vulnerability count as well as the severity-wise breakup of vulnerability.

The following scan information is captured in Nessus reports:

- Target IP address
- Target host name
- Target Mac address
- DNS name
- Scan start time
- Scan end time
- Target operating system

Some of the fields are shown in the following screenshot:

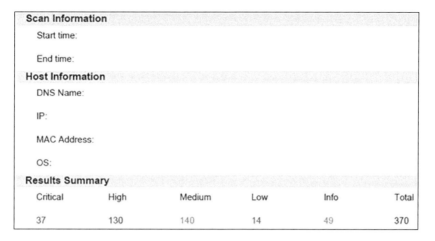

The Nessus report details the vulnerabilities found in a Nessus scan for the scanned hosts. This includes the following information about each vulnerability:

- Vulnerability against the plugin numbers
- Synopsis
- Description
- The **See Also** link about that vulnerability
- Solution
- Risk factor
- CVSS base score
- References
- Plugin information
- Exploit With
- Ports

The following screenshot shows a sample vulnerability with the details of a vulnerability shown in a Nessus-generated report:

10114 - ICMP Timestamp Request Remote Date Disclosure

Synopsis

It is possible to determine the exact time set on the remote host.

Description

The remote host answers to an ICMP timestamp request. This allows an attacker to know the date that is set on the targeted machine, which may assist an unauthenticated, remote attacker in defeating time-based authentication protocols.
Timestamps returned from machines running Windows Vista / 7 / 2008 / 2008 R2 are deliberately incorrect, but usually within 1000 seconds of the actual system time.

Solution

Filter out the ICMP timestamp requests (13), and the outgoing ICMP timestamp replies (14).

Risk Factor

None

References

CVE	CVE-1999-0524
XREF	OSVDB:94
XREF	CWE:200

Plugin Information:

Publication date: 1999/08/01, Modification date: 2012/06/18

Ports

icmp/0

```
The difference between the local and remote clocks is 2 seconds.
```

Report customization

In the previous section, we learned that the Nessus report captures a lot of details about each vulnerability report. At times, when you are engaged as a consultant for a Vulnerability Assessment report, you may not want to use the report generated by Nessus to share with the client since it has a lot of details about each vulnerability; this can be well understood by and useful for a security consultant, but not for an end customer who just needs to understand what the vulnerability is and what needs to be done to fix it. Another case may be that you want to showcase the report in a different format provided by the client; for that, you need to customize the report accordingly.

It is completely up to you what parameters you want to include in your Vulnerability Assessment report. A default report generated by Nessus is pretty good and comprehensive. It might happen that you also need to see ease of exploit in the report or maybe the effort required to fix the vulnerability. What to include and what not to include in the vulnerability report is totally up to the person who creates the report and the organization's requirement. You are required to customize the reports accordingly.

Customization can be done by removing specific fields from the default Nessus report and adding extra fields into it that you need in addition to the default fields. If you are required to create the report in the Microsoft Word format, you can copy and paste from the default reports generated by Nessus.

I recommend the following format for generating an impressive report:

- Report front page:
    - Name of the client
    - Assignment or project name
    - Report submitted by
- Document information page:
    - Document title
    - Version
    - Author's name
    - Reviewer's name
    - Approver's name
    - Document change history with dates
    - Document distribution list
    - Document data classification
- Header and footer on each page with data classification, page number, document name, logo of organization, and so on

- Executive summary:
    - ° A brief about the Vulnerability Assessment project with its scope
    - ° The vulnerabilities count with severity segregation
    - ° The graphical representation of critical, high, medium, low, and informative vulnerabilities with their count
    - ° The IP/vulnerability count graph
    - ° A table with the name of the vulnerability, risk rating, business impact, and link to details in the same report

- Details section:
    - ° Critical risk vulnerabilities
        - Name of the vulnerability
        - Vulnerability description
        - Business impact
        - Affected IP or application name
        - Artifact of exploit (optional)
        - Mitigation/recommendation
        - Prerequisite to mitigation
        - Patch name, if applicable to mitigate
        - Vulnerability reference links
        - CVE references
        - Nessus plugin information
        - Exploitable with (Metasploit, core impact, CANVAS, and so on)
        - Implementation steps
        - Implementation cost
        - Implementation complexity
        - Roll-back steps if mitigation is not successful
    - ° High-risk vulnerabilities
        - Same fields as mentioned under critical risk vulnerabilities

- ° Medium-risk vulnerabilities

     Same fields as mentioned under critical risk vulnerabilities

- ° Low-risk vulnerabilities

     Same fields as mentioned under critical risk vulnerabilities

- ° Informational vulnerabilities

     Same fields as mentioned under critical risk vulnerabilities

A penetration test report is a little different from the Vulnerability Assessment report. A penetration test report should also include a section on how to exploit the vulnerability with the evidence showing how it was exploited.

Report automation

The report automation section is not specific to Nessus; in general, the multiple Vulnerability Assessment tools available in the market and their older versions don't support the generation of reports in the Microsoft Excel or PDF formats. In order to make the most out of those autogenerated reports and to conform them with organizations' preferred reporting formats, mostly Excel or Word, scripts can be written to convert those default reports to generate reports for our own needs.

One other need for Nessus reports' automation is that while you integrate Nessus reports using different tools, such as Archer and Agiliance, which are governance risk and compliance tools; the security information and event management tool; or any other tools available in your organization using which you want Nessus to generate Vulnerability Assessment results. In these cases, for integration, every tool has certain prerequisite formats for reports. Most tools accept CSV formats. In order to convert reports to the desired formats, I recommend writing scripts.

Summary

This chapter covers reporting options in Nessus. The content of the Vulnerability Assessment report should be customized to suit the audience of the report, ranging from higher management to technical teams working on the closure of vulnerabilities. After completing the scan, the output is available under the **Result** tab in Nessus. Under this tab, we have the summary of hosts, the vulnerabilities found, and an option to export the results.

Results can be exported in different formats, such as PDF, CSV, and HTML, and Nessus offers five options to decide on the content to be included, namely **Hosts Summary (Executive)**, **Vulnerabilities by Host**, **Compliance Checks**, **Vulnerabilities By Plugin**, and **Compliance Checks (Executive)**. The **Result** tab also has a filtering option where the drop-down menu filters the required class and types of vulnerabilities and can be filtered from the overall output.

The report captures scan information along with vulnerability details, including the synopsis, description, solution, risks, plugins, the CVSS score, and other important details.

This chapter also covers report customization from an external consultant perspective and the kinds of details that should be captured in the report. Finally, the report automation concept was introduced; this can be done using scripts and also through integration with the GRC compliance tool or SIEM solutions.

5
Compliance Checks

Nessus is well-known as a vulnerability scanner, but it also provides the option to do compliance checks. Using this option, it can be cross-checked whether the secure configuration settings of an infrastructure, such as servers, network devices, database, and desktop, are in compliance with the defined policy or best practices an organization is following.

The compliance check audit is an important and necessary feature required as per the current security needs of an organization. All security-aware organizations define and implement secure configuration settings for their IT and network infrastructures to prevent them from being compromised by security threats that can be realized due to any misconfiguration. Also, such compliance requirements for security hardening and checking the implementation also arise because of regulatory requirements when a company has to adhere to different compliance regulations, such as ISO 27001 for a information security management system, HIPAA for the health industry, and SOX for a financial domain.

To check the compliance of servers, network devices against these defined controls, or a secure configuration, a regular compliance check activity is required. Conducting such compliance checks manually, especially when the size of the infrastructure is large, and even when post sampling and controls to be checked per device are large in number, will be a tedious and time-consuming job. This may also result in the possibility of errors and time consumed in a to-and-fro exchange between operation and compliance teams for the preparation, validation, and correction of artifacts.

The compliance check option offered by Nessus will help to conduct such a check in an automated manner. Nessus also offers options to modify the compliance files for them to be in line with an organization's device-hardening policies.

Vulnerability Scan will typically identify well-know vulnerabilities present in the system, for which a plugin is available, and will identify missing patches.

Auditing will check the compliance of the infrastructure with the secure configuration defined in the local policy.

Resulting less vulnerabilities during a vulnerability scan doesn't mean that the system is securely configured. For example, if the password policy of an organization mandates a minimum of 10 characters because it handles sensitive information, a server might have patches updated or have relatively less vulnerabilities in the output of a VA scan conducted. This is because the server will not ensure that a password policy of 10 characters is configured. This feature is available with Nessus professional feed.

Nessus compliance checks are available for major platforms such as server OSes (Windows and Unix), databases, desktops, and network devices, as well as audit standards such as PCI DSS.

This chapter will cover the following major areas:

- Audit polices
- How to configure the Nessus compliance check policy
- Compliance reporting in Nessus
- The compliance check option for different types of infrastructures

Audit policies

To conduct these compliance audits, policies are available in the files with the `.audit` extension, which are available for different infrastructure elements such as databases, Windows, and Cisco. These audit files also contain the common checkpoints covered under well-known standards such as SOX and PCI-DSS. These files also have recommendations from well-known security governance and advisory bodies such as NIST and CERT.

These audit files can be tweaked in line with the local policy or hardening documents. Tenable offers options to download these audit files from its support site and provides documentation to understand the syntax of these files to create them with customizations as per your requirements. Tenable also offers tools to convert a Windows policy file with the `.inf` extension to one with the `.audit` extension.

To enable the use of the compliance check option, an end user first needs to click on he **+ Add Policy**. The compliance check option is available under **Policies | Plugins Preferences**.

Out of the various Nessus plugins available, the plugin family of interest for a compliance check is **Policy Compliance**. This plugin check covers different infra components such as servers and the network.

The following screenshot shows the **Policy Compliance** plugin family:

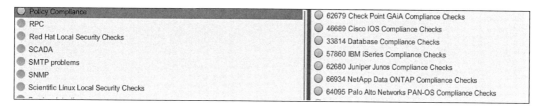

To use customized audit files, use the **Preferences** option under **Policies**. Under the **Preferences** tab, there is a drop-down menu to choose different compliance checks such as **Cisco IOS Compliance Checks** and **Database Compliance Checks**. Here, a user will also get an option to choose and upload more than one audit file that will be used to perform the compliance checks.

The following screenshot shows the **Database Compliance Checks** option selected:

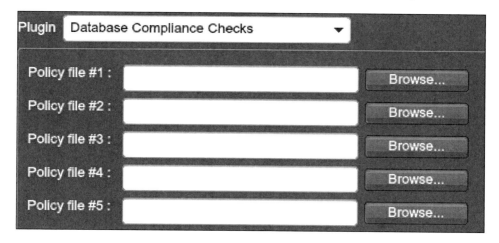

Credentials

For Nessus to do a compliance check, credentials should be provided for it to log in to the system to do local checks. The credentials used should be those of a privileged account, that is, a super user privilege in case of a Unix account with administrative privilege to read the local machine policy. In case of a database compliance check, database credentials will be required. In case of a Cisco IOS compliance check, the enable password is required to do a configuration audit. The credentials can be added under **Policies | Credentials** as it was done during the VA scanning.

The following screenshot is an example of how to provide credentials in case of a Cisco configuration audit:

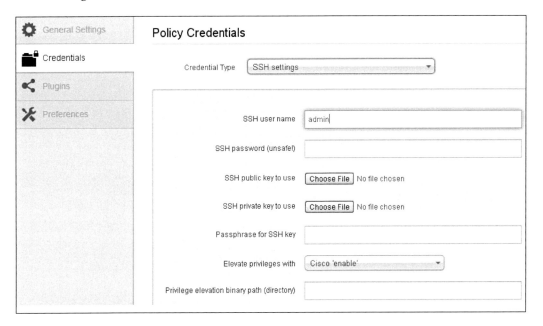

Compliance reporting

To get a report specific to the compliance status of the target in question, Nessus provides options such as **Compliance Check** and **Compliance Check (Executive)** while saving the report. Using any of these options, one can get the compliance status of the system against the controls as present in the `.audit` file. This is represented in the report by mentioning if the compliance has failed, passed, or skipped along with an executive summary. Inconclusive tests are reported under errors and warnings.

The following screenshot showcases the report generated using the **Compliance Check** and **Compliance Check Summary** options:

Auditing infrastructure

Compliance plugins are available under the **Policy Compliance** plugin family. This section lists the plugins available under this family, which showcase the kind of infrastructure for which a compliance audit can be done. For each type of infrastructure element, such as servers, networks, and databases, the appropriate policy file, credentials, and plugin needs to be selected as mentioned in the preceding sections in this chapter.

Windows compliance check

Using this plugin, one can check the compliance parameters set under the **Policies** option of the Windows framework. The examples of some of the checks conducted under Windows audit include the following:

- Registry setting
- File permissions
- Password policy
- Lockout policy

- Auditing policy
- User rights policy
- Service audits

Windows File Content

The **Windows File Content** option allows Nessus to check Windows file types (Excel, Adobe, or text files), which may contain sensitive data such as **Personal Identifiable Information** (**PII**) and credit card details.

Unix compliance check

Nessus can do a compliance check on different flavors of Unix such as Solaris, Red Hat, AIX, HP-UX, SUSE, Gentoo, and freebsd. Key checks include the following:

- Password management
- File permissions
- Password file management
- Permission management
- Root access management
- Running processes

Cisco IOS compliance checks

Using this plugin, a Cisco machine running a configuration file for Cisco IOS devices can be checked. Compliance checks can be done against saved, running, or startup configurations. Examples include the following:

- Access list applied to interfaces
- SNMP community strings are protected by ACLs
- Unrequited services are disabled
- An SNMP default community string is changed

Database compliance checks

Nessus can also check compliance of the different databases against security policies. Databases that are supported include MS SQL, Oracle, MySQL PostgreSQL, IBM DB2, and Informix/DRDA. To ensure the completeness of a report, the account used to log in to the database should have an SYSDBA or SA permission. Database compliance check plugins typically use SELECT queries to fetch security configurations from the database. Following are few examples:

- Checking for logins with no expiration details
- Checking if unauthorized stored procedures are enabled

PCI DSS compliance

Payment Card Industry Data Security Standard (PCI-DSS) is a well-known standard used for payment cards. Nessus offers PCI DSS compliance plugins to check the configuration against the requirement in this standard.

VMware vCenter/vSphere Compliance Check

The VMware vCenter/vSphere Compliance Check plugin uses the VMware SOAP API to audit ESX VMware, ESXi, and vCenter/vSphere virtualization software. Credential information to conduct an audit can be added to **VMware vCenter SOAP API Settings** in the **Advanced** section of a policy. Examples include the following:

- Missing patches
- Missing security updates

Some other platforms that are included in Nessus's compliance check options include the following (please cross-check the updated documentation on Tenable's official website, https://support.tenable.com/) A few sections of this chapter has been referenced from learning material available on Nessus website http://www.tenable.com:

- IBM iSeries compliance checks
- Juniper Junos compliance checks
- NetApp Data ONTAP compliance checks

- Palo Alto Network PAN-OS compliance checks
- Check Point GAiA compliance checks

 The compliance plugins are only available to professional feed customers.

Summary

Nessus provides options of doing automated compliance checks using the tool, apart from vulnerability scanning. Using this option, it can be cross-checked whether the secure configuration settings of the infrastructure such as servers, network devices, and databases are in compliance with the defined policy or best practices an organization is following. A compliance requirement is also derived from different compliance standards adhered to by an organization. This feature is available to professional feed subscribers.

The **Policy Compliance** plugin family is available for compliance check scanning. The plugin family includes, but is not limited to, servers, network devices, and standards such as PCI DSS. The Nessus **Results** tab also offers a **Compliance** option while saving the output to specifically generate a compliance report. These compliance checks can be modified by using the .audit files. Appropriate credentials of the underlying infrastructure on which a compliance audit is being performed need to be updated in the tool.

Index

Thank you for buying
Learning Nessus for Penetration Testing

About Packt Publishing

Packt, pronounced 'packed', published its first book "*Mastering phpMyAdmin for Effective MySQL Management*" in April 2004 and subsequently continued to specialize in publishing highly focused books on specific technologies and solutions.

Our books and publications share the experiences of your fellow IT professionals in adapting and customizing today's systems, applications, and frameworks. Our solution based books give you the knowledge and power to customize the software and technologies you're using to get the job done. Packt books are more specific and less general than the IT books you have seen in the past. Our unique business model allows us to bring you more focused information, giving you more of what you need to know, and less of what you don't.

Packt is a modern, yet unique publishing company, which focuses on producing quality, cutting-edge books for communities of developers, administrators, and newbies alike. For more information, please visit our website: www.packtpub.com.

Writing for Packt

We welcome all inquiries from people who are interested in authoring. Book proposals should be sent to author@packtpub.com. If your book idea is still at an early stage and you would like to discuss it first before writing a formal book proposal, contact us; one of our commissioning editors will get in touch with you.

We're not just looking for published authors; if you have strong technical skills but no writing experience, our experienced editors can help you develop a writing career, or simply get some additional reward for your expertise.

Instant Penetration Testing: Setting Up a Test Lab How-to

ISBN: 978-1-84969-412-4   Paperback: 88 pages

Set up your own penetration testing lab using practical and precise recipes

1. Learn something new in an Instant! A short, fast, focused guide delivering immediate results

2. A concise and clear explanation of penetration testing, and how you can benefit from it

3. Understand the architectural underpinnings of your penetration test lab

Advanced Penetration Testing for Highly-Secured Environments: The Ultimate Security Guide

ISBN: 978-1-84951-774-4   Paperback: 414 pages

Learn to perform professional penetration testing for highly-secured environments with this intensive hands-on guide

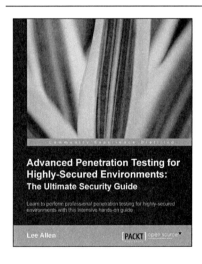

1. Learn how to perform an efficient, organized, and effective penetration test from start to finish

2. Gain hands-on penetration testing experience by building and testing a virtual lab environment that includes commonly found security measures such as IDS and firewalls

Please check **www.PacktPub.com** for information on our titles

PUBLISHING

**Metasploit Penetration Testing
Cookbook**

ISBN: 978-1-84951-742-3   Paperback: 268 pages

Over 70 recipes to master the most widely used
penetration testing framework

1. More than 80 recipes/practical tasks that will
   escalate the reader's knowledge from beginner
   to an advanced level

2. Special focus on the latest operating systems,
   exploits, and penetration testing techniques

3. Detailed analysis of third party tools based
   on the Metasploit framework to enhance the
   penetration testing experience

**Web Penetration Testing with
Kali Linux**

ISBN: 978-1-78216-316-9   Paperback: 342 pages

A practical guide to implementing penetration testing
strategies on websites, web applications, and standard
web protocols with Kali Linux

1. Learn key reconnaissance concepts needed as
   a penetration tester

2. Attack and exploit key features, authentication,
   and sessions on web applications

3. Learn how to protect systems, write reports,
   and sell web penetration testing services

Please check **www.PacktPub.com** for information on our titles

33717768R00066

Made in the USA
Middletown, DE
24 July 2016